Let prayer help you

Let prayer help you

By RUTH C. IKERMAN

Guideposts
Carmel, New York 10512

Dedicated to
Arlene and Gene Dawson,
faithful prayer companions of
Larry and Ruth Ikerman

All Scripture references are from
the Authorized King James Version.

This Guideposts edition is published
by special arrangement with
Christian Herald Books.

Library of Congress Cataloging in Publication Data
Ikerman, Ruth C.
Let prayer help you.
1. Prayer. I. Title.
BV210.2.I36   248'.3   79-24320
ISBN 0-915684-71-3

Contents

Preface

Each of my 15 devotional books has contained prayers for everyday use and special occasions, but this is the first time I have undertaken to write about prayer itself.

Perhaps I have hesitated because of a feeling that, just as you learn to write by writing, so you learn to pray by praying. Yet many times a writer can find help in a book about writing by applying its examples to personal writing projects.

So it is my sincere hope that somewhere in this book you will find fresh insight into how to solve your own prayer problems and build your own prayer patterns. In any case, the writing of it has given new impetus to my own prayer life, and for this I am grateful to God.

We live in a world that needs the warmth of fellowship which comes through praying, either alone or with friends and family. May God bless each reader, and may we undergird each other with the power of prayer. Together let us lift ourselves and our dear ones into the light of His healing love.

Ruth C. Ikerman

Introduction

I suspect that more books have been written about prayer than about any other resource for coping with day-to-day living. Why then another book?

For one thing, prayer is an inexhaustible subject. For another, it is intensely personal. For another, few of us feel that we are very good at it.

There are as many new things to say about prayer as there are praying people to say them. Ruth Ikerman does not write from a thunderous, cosmic, all-knowing point of view, as so many authors do when approaching a vast subject, but quietly, gently. Sharing her own prayer experiences and those of men, women and children she has met on her travels, she tells little stories, small incidents that others might miss. Because of her unusual sensitivity, they become parables through which life is interpreted and large meanings demonstrated. As someone has put

1

it, she "sees what everyone else has seen, and thinks what no one else has thought." That is the essence of writing—or of praying.

As you find your own way into prayer—perhaps self-consciously at first—it may help to keep in mind two words. Presence. Patience.

Prayer is presence, the assurance that Someone is there.

When I was a small boy, I slept in an attic room that seemed very far away from the rest of the house. I was always the first to be put to bed. My father or mother would take me up the stairs to the second floor, then up the stairs to the attic, tuck me in, turn out the light, and go downstairs again. As I heard the steps getting fainter, farther away, I became aware of the rattling dormer windows and the flickering shadows cast by the swaying street-light outside, and I was afraid.

One night my father said, "Would you rather I leave the light on, and go downstairs, or turn out the light and stay with you for a while?"

Of course I chose presence over light. The dark-ness did not matter if my father was there. Prayer is like that. It is not necessarily getting. It is knowing.

Then, patience. Not that we need to be patient with God, but that we need to understand how patient He must be with us. I have been grateful many times, in retrospect, that I did not receive things I prayed for. I once tried to get an editorial position on a magazine I thought was the greatest of the time. I prayed about this earnestly before and after an interview. When I did not get the job, I thought God had failed me when I needed Him. A few years later, the magazine went out of business. I had been disappointed with God for not getting me a ticket on the *Titanic!*

The important point to remember in praying is that God can see down the road farther than we can see. We parents listen lovingly to our children, but we do not give them everything they want.

As we are able, we do try to give them everything they need. God is like that. Prayer is like that. "If ye then . . . know how to give good gifts unto your children, how much more shall your Father which is in heaven give good things to them that ask him?" Good things. Good in the long run. Good when the implications and results and fallout are taken into account. God can see far ahead. We cannot.

May you find assurance and confidence in your own adventures in prayer. Let prayer help *you.*

Kenneth L. Wilson
Former Editor, *Christian Herald*

*"And all things, whatsoever ye shall ask in
prayer, believing, ye shall receive."*

Matthew 21:22

I/The Power We Can Trust

1/The glory of prayer

When we are children most of us learn some sort of prayer. It may be the simple "Now I lay me down to sleep," which a nurse recently told me was the prayer she often heard from the lips of the aged in the convalescent home where she works.

Perhaps it is a child's brief table blessing, such as "God bless this food and us," offered in beautiful innocence of the time and talent it has taken for parents to provide food for the table.

Somewhere along the years we often lose the ability to pray with such simplicity. Why should this be so? Perhaps because in this fast-moving, impersonal world we feel that it is an insult to God to ask Him to take care of the small details of our comparatively insignificant lives.

When I voiced this philosophy in the presence of

an older friend, he startled me by saying vigorously: "Be careful that you do not miss the glory of prayer. The greatness of God is proven by His infinite attention to the details of our prayers."

This caused me to stop to take notice of my casual words about prayer, for the speaker was a fine architect whose buildings still give beauty in southern California where many stores and homes have been razed in the name of progress.

He told me that as an architect, it was his task to decide what he wanted to build and to see it completed in his mind's eye, having an overall view of the project. Its success then hinged on his constant attention to the smallest detail.

In his view there were no small details. A slight mistake in one room, when duplicated, could create a giant variation in the entire building, and could even affect its relative location on the lot.

He faced me intently and said, "Do you think God is any less interested in your building a life than I am in completing a building?"

The question surprised me so much that I cannot remember how I answered, for he was a man with whom I had never before discussed religion. Now he told me that prayer undergirded his every project. He gave me a parting reminder: *Never be afraid to pray about little details.*

It took me a long time to accept his advice, for in this age of skepticism, we all think we are able to go it alone much of the time. We are ashamed to bother the God of the universe with little matters.

Yet the Bible says that God has an interest in even

the smallest matters: "Are not two sparrows sold for a farthing? and one of them shall not fall on the ground without your Father. But the very hairs of your head are all numbered" (Matthew 10:29, 30).

So the first thing we have to do in building a prayer life is to become humble enough to be willing to pray about little things. When this problem is overcome, it is possible to set up patterns of prayer that can be relied on for larger matters as well.

This is not an easy thing to do, but on it rests the potential for an abundant prayer life. The foundation of prayer is a succession of little prayers answered and thus forged into steel sturdy enough to withstand the shocks of life and all of its emotional storms.

How can we learn again to pray about the little things? Go back in your memory to the time when you stopped believing that God is interested in the simple things of your life. Was it when you were a teenager and some classmate scoffed at your prayer?

Does it go back even earlier to the time when a relative remarked that it was all right for a child to give a table blessing, but they didn't do such foolish things in their own home?

Maybe you persisted with your prayers into young adulthood, but stopped believing when a certain job or desire did not materialize even in answer to frequent prayer.

What is needed first is a return to the moment when you stopped trusting God with the little things. Then it is easier to get back on the roadway of prayer and start anew.

Nobody can walk a road without a map and some sense of destination, particularly when in new territory or in an area revisited after a long absence. So one of the most helpful tools in setting up a prayer life is the Bible.

Just pick it up and begin to read for as long a time as you have. Try to get into the sweep of the chapters, the panorama of the philosophy, as you do when reading a short story or a novel. When you stop to consider one verse over and over before you have an established background of Bible reading, it is easy to lose interest and miss the meaning. Perhaps one reason people cast aside church and its sermons is because they become bored with a lengthy explanation of one verse.

Let the whole Bible become the large map to inspire your heart as you return to prayer. When you find your own favorite passages, you will have a sense of reassurance that there is always something to which you can turn again and again for help in moments of discouragement.

The Bible points the way to the abundant life by the very human examples of men and women who failed, and who tried again, and perhaps failed over and over before reaching a new period of success, adjustment or adaptation.

Becoming familiar with the Bible is also one of the surest ways to reinforce an already active prayer life. Use your concordance to look up the special passages about prayer and become a part of the ageless and endless procession of those who have followed the glorious banners of prayer.

A PRAYER PATTERN _____

☐ Find a place where you can sit down quietly and be introspective for a few minutes. Try to think back to the exact moment when you first lost interest in prayer.

☐ If you have never prayed, try to discover why you have never entered into the fellowship of prayer.

☐ When you know your own perfectly good reasons for your own special problem, you are then in a position to take steps to change the situation.

> *Dear God, it is hard for me to believe*
> *that You truly care for me*
> *and are interested in my life.*
> *Yet I want to believe*
> *and I need Your help.*
> *So please*
> *accept this as a prayer asking*
> *for guidance.*
> *Show me how to believe in prayer*
> *and to set up patterns*
> *that will help me to live life*
> *more fully.*
> *I thank Thee for the promise that I*
> *am Thy child*
> *and can reach Thee through prayer.*
> *Amen.*

2/Prayer is universal

One of the things the traveler notices is the many different forms that prayer takes. Once when my husband and I were traveling around the world by freighter and bus, we found in almost every country some fresh evidence of the wish of the average man and woman to talk to God.

Walking the narrow streets of a little village in Japan, we came upon a prayer tree. A young woman was carefully tying little white rolls of paper to the twigs of the tree, using what seemed to be a mixture of ribbon and twine.

I could tell by the intense look on her face that this was a matter of immense importance in her life, even though I could not read a word of the Japanese that was affixed to the scroll.

A guide explained to me that as long as the piece

of paper remained on the tree, the young woman would believe that her prayer was being answered. When it fell to the ground she could affix another prayer: the same one if she were still interested in receiving an answer to the first problem, or a new one concerning some other development in her life.

Sometimes I have thought how nice it would be if I could find such an easy way of knowing whether my prayer was being answered or not, for occasionally the pattern is indistinct. Often we do not know until long after we have prayed the original prayer whether it was truly answered. Sometimes we are surprised and gratified at the far-reaching results from our earnest and humble prayers.

Another form of prayer is the prayer wheel, which the supplicant patiently turns again and again, as we saw in India. On one blistering hot afternoon, the sun bore down relentlessly but the man in the white robe and turban never stopped in his self-imposed task of endlessly turning the prayer wheel.

My husband and I were wiping the perspiration from our faces, but he kept on steadily at his dedicated work with the prayer wheel. The guide explained that this constant motion kept the prayers in circulation, so they had a better chance of being answered happily.

He said further that, if I were interested, I could hire a man to turn a prayer wheel for me; there would be virtue in this act as long as my prayers were affixed to the wheel.

That, in essence, seems to be what some of us like to do—rely on someone else to do the prayer work because it does take hard work to pray our own prayers in certain circumstances. When the going is rough, we may not even know how to phrase our prayers. It is hard to keep them in motion, when so many daily tasks must be completed at home, school or business.

The wish to find answers to prayers is almost universal among all peoples, no matter what means they use to express the prayers. Often, beautiful prayer shrines are erected, perhaps with the thought that the lovely surroundings will add to prayer's effectiveness. In Singapore we were taken by our guide to one such building where he and his family worshipped.

Beautiful white water lilies with yellow and pink centers floated in a pond lined with blue tiles. The flashing bodies of brilliant large goldfish sparkled in the spring sunlight. From the pool, white steps led upward into the area for prayer. In the center of this room was an altar made of mother-of-pearl. Reverently our guide went toward it, and bowed his head in an attitude of prayer. Walking on tiptoe in the hush of the lovely room, my husband and I joined him there, silently voicing our own prayer requests.

Uppermost in my heart that day were the Chinese orphan children in Hong Kong with whom we had recently visited at the Christian Children's Home. We had shared with them their simple meal of rice and fruit and could recall the echo of their musical voices as they said their thanks in a table grace.

Later we had spoken to them through an interpreter, and one little boy had raised his hand. The translator said he wanted us to promise we would "please remember always to pray for peace, so we can grow up without war." The memory of this request lingered with us as we continued our journey.

Aboard the freighter on Sunday mornings, some of the crew would read from the Scriptures, as we did, sitting in the lounge with its big windows looking out to the ocean, sunlight and passing clouds.

The Bible we carried is a favorite now, for one marked passage tells the date of the lovely morning we passed through the China Sea. We watched the flying fish, "the butterflies of the sea," as they emerged from the water into the air and then dove back into their watery home.

It was a moment of such intense beauty that the very earth and sea seemed to be worshipping. As I watched the scene, my mind suddenly shifted to the flight of the hummingbirds at home when I was a child. The whitecaps on the sea became the little white church with its tall steeple where I first repeated prayers in unison with my playmates.

In that moment, my heart seemed to be both at home and in this distant place, and all bound up in the prayers of eternity. I knew that prayer is indeed a universal hope and longing of all people, and I was refreshed and renewed in my desire to always remain in an attitude of believing in prayer.

Why is it so hard for us to believe, when we have the evidence that prayer is a universal hope and attitude? Probably in large part it's because of unanswered prayers, but we should find strength in remembering the universal aspects of prayer.

This universality is made evident whenever one visits the beautiful Pater Noster Church on the Mount of Olives in Jerusalem. There the words of the Lord's Prayer are written in many different languages on colored tiles that form the aisles leading into the church. On the morning we visited there, we heard tourists reading aloud in their own languages, and now we often remember that moment for its beauty and for its message of mankind's universal need.

A PRAYER PATTERN

☐ Pick out the unanswered prayer that bothers you the most. Commit it to God once more in prayer, and ask for wisdom to see the emerging answer.

☐ Remember that prayer is a universal act of the heart, and promise yourself and God that you will keep on praying a little bit each day.

☐ Recognize your common humanity with people of all races and religions who turn to prayer for answers and release.

> *Dear Father, forgive me*
> *for having pulled away from prayer*
> *which is so universal.*
> *Restore to me the joy of fellowship*
> *with the many who continue to pray*
> *in spite of handicaps*
> *or discouragement.*
> *May we all grow in grace through daily*
> *prayers for peace and harmony*
> *in Thy beautiful world.*
> *Grant us the strength which comes from*
> *sharing our common needs,*
> *hopes*
> *and dreams*
> *through the universal impact*
> *of prayer.*
> *Amen.*

3/The most – not the least

One morning when I was selling paint in the store owned by my husband and myself, an acquaintance stopped by and said: "I am sorry your husband is in the hospital. I want you to know I am praying for him. That is the least I can do."

He wanted a small purchase, a can of fire-engine red enamel to use in painting his grandson's wagon. As I slipped it into a brown paper sack, he asked me to be sure to give his greetings to my husband.

A few minutes later he was back at the counter. "I want to correct an impression I made a few minutes ago," he told me. "I said prayer was the least I could do for you and your husband. What I should have said was that it is the *most* I can do for you both."

With that he turned with a warm smile on his face and at the door stopped to wave. He had returned on a busy morning to make clear his position about the importance of prayer. It took a while for me to truly appreciate this position, but now I know how right it is, and what a rich gift were his words.

Prayer now seems to me always the most we can do in any baffling situation, no matter how many medical or legal experts we may have called in to help us solve the problem. How can any of us possibly see the outcome? How can we know what is best? Which road shall we take?

We need a power we can trust to know these things, and to see over and beyond the point at which we are stopped at the present. If we cannot turn to God in prayer at such times, where indeed can we turn?

The statistics about alcohol, drugs and suicide show that those who have turned elsewhere surely have not found the answer. Sometimes we become discouraged when we pray and think that we do not have the answer either. If we become bitter and turn away completely, then there is no possibility of receiving an answer. For first we must ask in prayer, and this gives us power in hope.

Often the answer comes after a long period of waiting. It is as though the answer has been there all the time, but we have not recognized it until some significant moment of prayer has shown us that the problem itself has dissolved as time has worked its healing ministry.

In such moments I remember with gratitude the customer who reminded me "prayer is the most."

Sometimes children seem to understand prayer

best. I think of the little girl who came into my hospital room once when I was recovering from an auto accident and said, "I brought you something besides these roses—you can have all of my prayer tonight. I don't need it for myself today."

With disarming simplicity the child told me that her little world seemed to be all right at the moment, and she could give all of her prayer to somebody in a hospital room. She understood that after an automobile accident an adult might need it. Her generous gesture touched me deeply. Instinctively she knew that prayer was the "most," even more than the lovely roses she had picked from her family's garden.

I have often wondered how she said her prayers that night, or if she just walked away and left them in my room for me to use. For I did rely on them and they made me feel better and more hopeful.

Another memorable evening, I learned what it is like not to be able to say prayers, but to have to depend on those we love to pray for us. In a never-to-be-forgotten moment, I was invited to witness the prayer period of a retarded child. She was home from the center where she lived and attended special school during the week.

The parents invited me into the bedroom of their adored little girl. She kneeled beside them, hid her face in her hands, and waited quietly. The father spoke: "God, our little girl cannot give Thee her praise in words, but we know she loves Thee, and we want to thank Thee for the blessings of this week. So hear our thanks to Thee for our daughter and for all who care for her. Keep her safe through another week, and guide those who feed her, teach her, and play with her. We bring her little friends to Thee and ask for Thy blessing on them and their families."

The little girl had been taught to say "Amen," and while her other words are not always distinguishable, this word came out clear and distinct. (Often I hear its loving echo when in a church service in my hometown, far removed from her distant home by the sea. The rhythm in her "Amen" reminds me of the sound of the waves hitting the shore, telling us again of God's great earth and our small time in which to enjoy it.)

The melodies of eternity were in the little girl's room when she uttered her "Amen." Surely this family knew that praying was the most they could do in this situation, which would sorely try the hearts of many. Without this kind of faith, it would be easy to turn away from prayer in the face of similar physical, mental or emotional problems.

Clinging to the belief that prayer is "the most" may be all that we are able to do, even when we cannot voice the prayers themselves. This is another way of defining faith, which surely is founded in prayer that links us to God the Father Almighty.

There are opportunities in our daily lives to give our testimony, just through continued prayer on any seemingly impossible situation. Who wants to settle for the least when there is available to us prayer as the most we can do for ourselves and for others?

A PRAYER PATTERN _____

□ Pick out an apparently hopeless situation in your life or that of some member of your family. Examine the attitudes you may have been carrying in your heart toward the situation. See if you can elevate this from a "least" to a "most" through some positive prayer.

□ One good way to reinforce your attitude is to make a list of prayers, and cross off each petition as the answer comes. Start your list today by remembering some moment of God's goodness from the past, and use this to build for a faith-filled future.

> *Father, help us to stand up*
> > *to the hard situations of life*
> > *by knowing that we always have*
> > *a mighty weapon at hand.*
> *We do not have to build*
> > *from our weakness*
> > *and think that the least we can do*
> > *is to try to pray.*
> *Instead we may succeed in Thy might*
> > *by recognizing that prayer*
> > *is the most we can do*
> > *since it links us to eternity*
> > *through Thee.*
> *Please hear our petitions in behalf*
> > *of ourselves and those we love*
> > *that we may be led to serve Thee better.*
> *In Thy name we pray,*
> > > *Amen.*

4/The corners you can't see around

When I opened the envelope, out fell a sheet of tablet paper on which a few words were written in pencil. This proved to be such a precious letter that I have saved it to re-read many times in the years since.

The letter was in response to a prayer of mine, first printed in a magazine, and later reprinted in book form with other prayers. The particular prayer was called "Waiting at the School Bus Corner."

The writer of the letter was a woman from a farming area in the Midwest. She told me that she was the driver of a school bus, taking children from their farm homes to the community schoolhouse. She said that she had never wanted to drive a school bus, and had never expected to do so, but the man who had held the job for many years had moved away.

Because she loved children and wanted them to be able to go to school, she had studied and passed the school bus tests.

"Somebody had to do it, so I prayed about it," she told me.

It had seemed right to her that she should volunteer, even though it was not convenient to be away from her own chores. She told me that she had read my prayer, and realized that she could pray about such a matter, particularly about her fears concerning the safety of the children.

Then she wrote a profoundly moving sentence that has helped me over many rough spots. "There is one corner I can't see around and I use your little prayer in the morning, always asking God to help me around that special corner."

What a marvelous testimony to the great opportunity that prayer affords us all! For life is just full of corners that none of us can see around. You can't leave the bus of life parked in some backyard; it has to keep on moving on its living journey, which each of us makes from birth to death. Often we panic at the thought of all the curves, but we can be as wise as the woman at the school bus wheel who began to pray about the corner she couldn't see around.

She told me that the time came when she could approach it without her heart pounding and her fingers trembling, and she thus became a better driver and more useful to her young charges.

Responsibility had plunged her into a difficult situation, but she used it to make her own life stronger, and to anchor her faith more securely in God's ability to help her, through the use of prayer.

Her words have stayed with me in writing articles and books, in working out the problems of a businesswoman and in dealing with family illness. Realistically, she reminded me of the corners we all face in our lives, with no possibility of seeing around them.

Will this loved one recover from his illness? Can we possibly face up to the inevitable ending of the life of an aged relative? If we don't know where the money is coming from for a child's education, can we find a way to round the financial corner?

Sometimes it is not just corners that we can't see around. The entire road may appear to be blocked by a problem that looms like a big wall. When any matter seems that large, I like to rely on that wonderful verse, "For by thee I have run through a troop: and by my God have I leaped over a wall" (Psalm 18:29).

This was David's way of saying that he had discovered God would provide the necessary energy for him to leap over the wall rather than climb fearfully, brick by brick. He had learned that difficulties could be conquered with God's help.

Corners we can't see around can disappear as we become stronger and walk toward them without fear. The corners that remain in our lives, and from which we sometimes hide in confusion, are the ones of which we are so afraid that we feel we cannot push on toward them.

Wise was the woman who realized that if she prayed about the corner, she could approach it with more strength. There is no problem in anyone's life that cannot be approached in this same trusting spirit.

Committing financial corners to God in prayer can remind us of fresh resources. Such a resource does not have to be monetary—perhaps just a reminder of a healthy body, which is capable of undertaking a second job to bring in more funds.

If the problem is the lack of a job, prayer sometimes can bring into consciousness a fresh recognition of one's true talents and career desires. Many a new business has been built on the realization that talents can be better expended.

Making use of adult education classes can help to expand these talents. This was proved by a young woman who used her day off from her job to take a class in cake decorating. Soon she was spending her weekends making cakes for children's parties, having fun designing circus or football cakes.

Ultimately, she decided she didn't wish to pursue this professionally, but the fun she enjoyed with her new hobby gave her fresh enthusiasm for her old job. She found she was looking at it with a positive point of view because the supplementary job had given her a new perspective.

When you pass the original corner and look back on it, the corner has a completely different shape. Sometimes it looks even larger than you remembered and you wonder again how you ever managed to get around it. More often it seems not to have been so very large after all.

When you walk on toward any of life's corners with faith, you will find the road becomes more approachable. Soon you are able to see around the corner, and get a clear vision of what beckons on the road ahead in happy future years.

A PRAYER PATTERN

☐ Try to think of the most prevailing fear you have as just a corner you can't presently see around. Is it fear of failing? Then try little by little to build a success in some familiar field. The old saying is true: Nothing succeeds like success. It may be just a tiny success, but if it is in a field that matters to you, the confidence can carry over into success in other fields.

☐ Make this a matter of prayer for growing confidence.

> *Dear God, forgive us our fearfulness*
> *about the corners of life.*
> *Help us to march forward psychologically*
> *and not retreat into dark corners*
> *of fearfulness and hopelessness.*
> *Lead us*
> *into the sunlight around the corner*
> *which temporarily hides from us*
> *the beauty of Thy universe*
> *and the joy of accomplishment.*
> *We pray in Thy great name,*
> *God of the Universe.*
> *Amen.*

"*Evening, and morning, and at noon, will I*
pray . . .and he shall hear my voice."

Psalm 55:17

II/Building Prayer Patterns

5/First clear your mind and heart

young friend who had fallen out of the habit of prayer said to me one day with great wistfulness, "I would like to start praying again, but I don't know how to begin."

This was the moment when I could pass along to someone else some of the very best advice about prayer I had ever received. An older friend had once said to me, "First clear your mind and heart."

At the time, I didn't understand the meaning of her words, and my face must have showed this ignorance. For with explicit kindness she explained what she meant by this phrase—a phrase that has proven most helpful in my prayer journey.

Apparently the first thing to do was to go apart for a time of meditation. This friend had an old chair that she found extremely comfortable, particularly when she put her feet on a footstool to rest while she meditated. Usually she started with a favorite Bible verse, often from memory but sometimes from her daily reading. This she might supplement with a po-em about a flower, or a bit of current philosophy "to take my mind off grief or worry."

She felt it was most important to take time to get in a mood to pray. Physical exercise helped her to become relaxed, and she stressed that these exer-cises did not need to be complicated.

"Just move your arms high above your head, or drop your hands to the side. It even helps to stretch your fingers apart." This latter I could readily be-lieve, as it usually proves an effective release from tension after long sessions at the typewriter.

Some of the other things she suggested included shaking both wrists and letting your fingers hang loosely toward the floor. It is also beneficial to let your head drop forward with your chin coming close to your chest in order to relax the back neck muscles.

Shake your head from side to side, as if to brush away negative thoughts. Then nod it up and down in the familiar "yes" motion to gain complete relaxa-tion before seeking spiritual guidance.

All of these simple exercises, she pointed out, can be done while sitting in the meditation chair. They help create a relaxed climate for cultivating the right mental attitude to both ask and receive in prayer.

Thus fortified with physical advice, I asked my friend what came next, and she said, "An attitude of thanksgiving is one of the best ways to become ready to receive more blessings."

Now as I recalled this good advice and passed it along to my own young friend, I reflected on how often it had helped me to bring into being some fresh blessing for which my heart was yearning. Only when I was aware of all the good that I already possessed was it possible to receive more blessings.

In recent years a whole school of thought has been built around the feeling that thanksgiving through praise results in effective answers to prayers. Many people advocate praying by the use of the simple phrase "Praise the Lord." Repeated often, this phrase helps you to concentrate on the power of God and His goodness, and clears the mind for proper petition and action.

The attitude of thanksgiving and praise makes the heart solidly aware of blessings already received. This creates an aura of positive feelings into which more good can be assimilated. If "like attracts like," then it follows that praying in a negative frame of mind can bring about more negative situations.

This reminds me of an acquaintance who commented about a very negative person in the community by saying, "I really don't want her to pray about my problem. I have trouble enough as it is."

How sad it seemed to me that the woman to whom she referred had such a reputation for a negative attitude that others were fearful of her offers of spiritual help. But it was true that, even in prayer, this woman seemed to thrive on details about sorrow and illness.

Effective prayer tries to erase such details from

the thought pattern. Instead, it is a part of effective prayer to concentrate joyously on pictures of the person in good health, or going to the bank to deposit a new paycheck.

When the deep desires of the heart are held firmly in prayer, energy is somehow freed to realize these dreams. A positive attitude prepares the mind to recognize opportunities and receive answers relating to the life of the individual.

"The man or woman who wants a job must visualize going to work day by day, and not just sit at home waiting for the telephone to ring," an employment counselor once told me.

Admittedly, this becomes increasingly hard to do when the application blanks are only acknowledged with a formal note, or perhaps not replied to at all. This is when endurance through prayer helps the individual keep away negative thoughts.

Each of us has the opportunity to discover our own best way to clear the mind and heart for prayer seeking positive answers. Some may find it in energetic walking or running. A rancher who had a successful prayer life once told me in a moment of sharing that he loved the quiet time he spent alone among his orange trees, for it gave him a chance to get his spiritual house in order.

Whatever technique we adopt, we have the example of Jesus and His disciples as mentioned in Mark 6:32: "And they departed into a desert place by ship privately." It is not an act of cowardice to run away when problems pile up. Rather it may be one of great intelligence and wise discipline to take a "mini-vacation" from problems, and find time for prayer.

How else do doctors face their heavy loads, if not to get away from the telephone for a weekend while someone "covers" for them? All of us need to learn to get away from pressing situations by going into the garden and looking at a flower, or watering a plant at the window sill. Whatever clears our mind and heart of tension is preparing the way for positive prayer.

A PRAYER PATTERN

☐ Within the limits of your own daily routine, experiment with the best way to be alone with your thoughts for a few minutes. You owe yourself this in preparation for meditation. Is your chair positioned so that the light shines too much in your eyes? Then move to a more comfortable spot. Does another window have a more peaceful view? Decide such small issues before proceeding to the larger matters of prayer.

> *Dear God, still my heart and mind*
> *so that earthly problems*
> *may be forgotten momentarily.*
> *Make me even temporarily realize*
> *that I am a part*
> *of the larger plan of eternity.*
> *Enlarge my mind to appreciate*
> *the great scope of Thy universe.*
> *In this moment*
> *I acknowledge Thy power*
> *and ask Thee to help me*
> *to learn to accept and apply it*
> *to my own problems.*
> *Humbly I wait*
> *in meditation and prayer*
> *for insight from Thee.*
> *Amen.*

6/ A prayer goal

Why is it that, often, people who realize they must have a goal to succeed in life think it is somehow wrong to set up a definite prayer goal?

Is it because we have been taught to pray for spiritual blessings in abstract, and think it wrong for us to ask for more definite items? Yet Jesus was a realist who faced life as He found it. When a community did not wish to welcome His disciples, He advised them to " . . . shake off the dust of your feet" (Matthew 10:14). He recognized the realities of life and always continued with His prayer life.

Why should we hesitate to ask God for that which we feel will add to our happiness? Where did the idea come from that we must be miserable supplicants, asking for help only in sorrow or danger?

Recently a young woman came to me and said: "I

am so lonely, but I don't like the men I meet. I wish I knew how to find some better companionship."

She was almost overcome with laughter when I asked in all sincerity, "Have you ever prayed about this situation?" It seemed logical that such an attractive young woman should have the escort she wanted. If God is her Heavenly Father, as I believe He is, then why shouldn't she ask for what she wants?

Her giggle indicated to me that she really did not believe that her goal could be reached, and that she did not want to rely on spiritual help. But without it, I did not know what I could do to help, for she had already tried going to clubs and hobby groups and she was bored with the young men she found in her church contacts.

It seemed to me that it might be possible to set up a prayer goal, if she could define her needs in simple terms: "God, please help me to find the right person so we may set up a Christian home."

I knew that if she began to pray this prayer she would soon find that her goal had to be modified. It might later become: "God, please make me the kind of person the right man will find."

Then the project may move forward with greater intensity. As her interests change she may be led into a group or a new set of surroundings that will help her meet her goal.

Just defining what it is you want can be of great help in spurring your prayer life into action. And there is a double advantage in such specific prayer, because inevitably the material goal merges into the spiritual goals.

Sometimes the situation gets worse before it gets any better, because answers may come in mysterious ways. I remember a combination of family circumstances that led me to pray for the gift of patience.

What happened? Things became a lot worse, calling for much more restraint on my part, much handling of my temper, and greater discipline in carrying out daily duties.

Finally, in the still of the night I saw that my prayer had indeed been answered. I had been given the gift of patience, but it had been developed through the piling on of problems that could only be solved by the exercise of *more* patience. I realized that I should be more careful in what I asked for when setting up future goals. In fact, an old adage warns, "Better be careful what you ask God for, as you will be sure to get it."

The responsibility rests with the individual to set up a prayer goal. Do you want to have a better marriage? Then tell God so, and ask for wisdom to see the problems and find the proper answers. Do you want to go back to school, and need money? If you pray about this, the chances are good that you will suddenly see a way to economize, or know where to secure the necessary funds. Without preparation through prayer, you may encounter many unnecessary roadblocks.

Friends of ours with a mentally retarded child faced the agonizing decision of whether to keep the child at home or place her in a school. Their prayer goal for the year was to be enabled to make the right decision.

As they prayed, our friends seemed to be led to new books concerning the situation, which led to the trying of new medication under their doctor's supervision. A cure was not achieved, but there was considerable improvement. They learned of a local organization of parents who were trying to help each other face this heartache, and through participation, found some of their own answers.

Without their prayer goal, they felt they would not have been guided to this supplementary material and warm fellowship. Ultimately, the decision was made to place the child in a newly-established home that they had heard about from other parents.

Their next prayer goal became one of asking for strength to meet the separation and to prepare the child for the change in environment. For the one essential fact about prayer goals is that the answering of one leads to the setting up of another.

Prayer is an ongoing chain of progression from one problem to another, and this is itself in the providence and wisdom of God. For it means that the individual need never feel alone, no matter what problem looms on the horizon.

Prayer is always there to provide spiritual companionship along the way. Therefore, any problem can be attacked and a goal set up for its solving.

Of course we don't want problems and all of the pain that they sometimes cause. But prayer is available to help find the solution, if a goal can be defined. The simplest way to reach answers is to set up a prayer goal. Anyone can learn how to do this by praying daily about life concerns.

A PRAYER PATTERN _____

☐ Stop letting your mind run in circles. Sit down and try to find the center of your current problem.

☐ Write down a goal. At first it will probably be five times as long as it needs to be.

☐ Try to reduce it to a summarizing sentence. Keep trying until you have 10 words, or even five. Then you can approach the problem by praying for your specific prayer goal.

☐ Persist until you have the answer.

Dear Heavenly Father, let us know the joy
of working with Thee
through our prayer goals.
So many little things come up in life
to keep us from making the
best progress
toward our central goal
of living a Christian life.
Give us wisdom
to break down the problems into goals
that will challenge us to do
our human best.
We depend upon Thy divine help,
even as we pray now in Thy name.
Amen.

7/Listen to
that inner voice

Often prayer is composed of asking, with no time allowed for just plain listening for an answer. It is a joyous moment when we learn how to listen to the inner voice and the promptings of the Holy Spirit.

In recent years, this third part of the Holy Trinity has often been identified with "far-out" experiences, which are at variance with many intellectual attitudes and points of view. Yet in its simplest definition, that of the companion who stays with us during our earthly journey, the Holy Spirit is the welcome and ever-present inner voice that can guide and lead us into pathways of service.

Many commonplace circumstances become spiritual adventures and add zest to our daily living. It is gratifying to discover that when we listen to the Holy Spirit, we are led into refreshing new experiences. Through such experiences I have come to a new understanding of the Holy Spirit.

On the occasions when I have felt most fruitful in my prayer life, the number of incidents that go beyond "coincidence" increases. I have come to feel that the inner voice of the Holy Spirit was indeed guiding me because I had asked in deep humility and listened as carefully as I was able to in spite of daily distractions.

Sometimes the telephone will ring just as we are thinking of an individual who lives many miles away, and here is the familiar, well-loved voice, calling because of an insistent inner nudge. Then again it may be an occurrence during a shopping expedition or trip to the library.

One busy noon hour recently, I parked in a downtown parking lot, pushed for time to finish the errands on my list. Because the morning had been frantic and I was rushing to an afternoon appointment, I paused for just a minute to catch my breath. Then I remembered that I must take time to listen and remain sensitive to the voice of the Holy Spirit.

This was in line with my prayer plan and self-made promise to truly try to listen for guidance. As I stood there by the car, preparing to lock the door, I said a little prayer to myself: "Forgive me, God, for all this rushing. Please plan my afternoon better."

I needed to cash a check, so I started toward the bank, but felt a strong impulse to go into the stationery store nearby where I love to browse. I had planned to skip this, but I was drawn there after my simple prayer.

Intent on listening to the inner voice, I entered the store. At the back counter stood the owner, one of my close friends; she was speaking to her customer, a mutual friend. They both burst into laughter at the sight of me, and thrust a pen into my hand.

It seemed that the customer had come to buy one of my books as a gift and was disappointed that the autographed copies were all sold. She said she had just been wondering if there was time to go to my home, or have the store owner telephone me to come down, when I walked in the door.

Here I was, happy to autograph the book where it could be wrapped and prepared for mailing. The three of us had a pleasant chat while I performed the little task, and later I reflected on how close I had come to missing this lovely moment of fellowship.

By listening to that inner voice, I had been able to accommodate two friends in a purchase that was enjoyable for me, also. An answered prayer always benefits everyone—not just the one who asks, but those who are in any way involved with the answer.

The benefits that come from listening to the Holy Spirit's voice cannot be measured. Sometimes the inner voice indicates that even a prayer focus itself should be changed, to ensure a better goal and a more inclusive answer.

In one listening session, I was told by that loving inner voice of the Holy Spirit to pray for help in arranging the daily patterns of my life. Often I seemed to run into difficulties, which could have been avoided if I had taken a minute for prayer, asking for the channels to be cleared for right action.

So now I try to listen and ask to be slowed down when the pace seems to become too hectic. Marvelous are the answers!

In typing this chapter, I was interrupted by a telephone call from my doctor's secretary. Could she change my afternoon's appointment from 2:30 to 3:30? It would accommodate an out-of-town patient if I could do this. I could hardly say yes quickly enough, for I needed more time at the desk, and in the back of my mind I had been wishing the appointment were later in the day. I had taken time to listen to the inner voice of the Holy Spirit early that morning when I had asked for special help with the day's timing of my activities. And as my own pattern changed, the way was made smoother for another person, in line with the universal truth that prayer answers do benefit all who are involved.

Such seemingly small incidents can have larger consequences when they serve to enlarge our faith, and they remind us of the blessed presence of the Holy Spirit as a divine companion along the earthly way of chores and daily duties.

This power is available to help us, without our straining and pushing, and without a feeling of tension. In fact, the inner voice is far more likely to be heard when we try to relax and just let the power come through into our daily lives. A sense of happy adventure comes into daily routine when there is the possibility of chance encounters that seem far more than coincidental. When we listen to that inner voice, we link ourselves to an essential part of God's eternal plan for our lives.

A PRAYER PATTERN

□ Try to empty your mind of the concerns of the day—the matching of thread to a piece of cloth, or finding the right swimsuit. Draw a deep breath and try to empty your mind of all thoughts of chores.

□ Think of the magnitude of the universe and the magnificence of God, and ask for His mighty power in daily contacts.

God of the Universe, forgive us for forgetting
that Thou art also the God
of the little things in life.
We thank Thee
for the blessing of the inner voice
as a companion in our humanity.
Make our paths smoother
as we listen for guidance
and as we try to live
in harmony with Thee
and with others.
We are open to daily demonstrations
of the power available to us
through prayer.
                    Amen.

8/Forgiveness
and the promise

Sometimes when prayers are not answered we begin to look around for reasons for our failures. No matter how much we may rationalize and make excuses, one reason for lack of success may be obvious—we have failed to forgive others and also to forgive ourselves.

An uncharitable attitude of revenge against someone is like a dead weight on the heart. Our own sense of guilt over the way we have involved someone in an upsetting experience also may limit our effectiveness. Isn't it entirely reasonable that dead weights can hold down our prayers, and keep them from ascending to the throne of God?

The Bible says, "And when ye stand praying, forgive, if ye have aught against any; that your Father also which is in heaven may forgive you your trespasses" (Mark 11:25).

47

This is followed by verse 26, which many cast aside lightly, but which says, "But if ye do not forgive, neither will your Father which is in heaven forgive your trespasses."

Most of us eventually realize how much we stand in need of forgiveness, perhaps for what we have done by an idle word. We weep for muffed opportunities in the past and the sorrow created in the present, and are afraid of the future. The first thing we need to do is to recognize that we owe it to ourselves, to those we have harmed and to God to keep on trying, always relying on His granting of more grace for the future.

Many people protest the Bible verse that stresses the necessity of forgiveness, feeling that the God of love would not refuse to forgive just because one human cannot manage to forgive another. Yet this controversial verse is positive in its appeal.

Jesus was telling His disciples that the easy way to pray is with a forgiving heart. Then there is no division within the soul; the heart does not have to carry heavy baggage on life's daily journeys.

A friend expresses it well when he says, "Enough trouble will catch up with you in this lifetime without your looking for it." He feels that failure to forgive is one of the best ways to look for trouble.

If the matter about which you are praying seems to have no answer, now is a good time to sit down and see what grudges you are holding and against whom. Many times a name will come to the surface immediately, without any inner prompting. Other times it may take some digging to discover what is nagging at us and depleting us of spiritual energy that might be better spent in active prayer.

Holding grudges always hinders action, and having hurt feelings may keep us from making the physical progress we should. For example, witness how much easier it is for hospital patients to get well when they like the doctor and the nurses. If some of the hospital staff seem unpleasant, patients may waste energy disliking them, energy that might better be spent in learning how to walk again.

The same is true in the inner world of personal prayer. Once any source of resentment is found, the next act should be one of silent forgiveness. Perhaps it can be disposed of by saying to yourself: "That was a long time ago. Why should it hurt me so now? Please take it away, Lord, and don't let me ever think of it again."

Such a simple, sincere statement as this can release energy for praying successfully for current needs. Perhaps it is a matter that needs to be set straight with a friend. If we do not take advantage of the present time to write a note, the opportunity may pass and it may forever be too late to make amends.

Or it may be that we need to go to see a friend to try to seek forgiveness for a real or imagined wrong. I remember how hurt and baffled I was when I heard others talking about anticipating a certain silver wedding anniversary celebration to which my husband and I were not invited. How could my good friend possibly do this to me? Then I reflected that this action was so unlike her gracious self that perhaps I had offended her by some remark or action.

I made myself ring her doorbell in humility, even though my pride kept arguing: What if she thinks you are begging for an invitation? She greeted me affectionately and said: "I was afraid you were ill, because I don't have your acceptance to our party."

When I explained my errand, she handed me her list with my name near the top. Then she said, "I'd never have forgiven myself if our friendship had broken up because of this." How glad I was that I had gone to see her, for not until well after the party date did the lost invitation arrive in our mail.

Simplicity lies at the heart of forgiveness. And the longer the act of forgiveness is delayed, the harder it becomes psychologically to make reparation. I am reminded of the advice I received as a young newspaper reporter from an editor who said, "Never bang any doors on the way out, as you may want to go back in again."

Isn't this the essence of forgiveness: To keep the doors of life swinging freely, open to both old and new opportunities of fellowship?

Forgiveness involves our entry into heaven, and it opens the doorway to successful praying on earth. The very act of prayer can be a useful tool in forgiveness. Are your feelings hurt? Do you feel as if you are being overlooked? Do you think someone is taking advantage of you? Then commit the matter to God in prayer. Ask to be made stronger than the problem. Seek psychological growth that will take you over the situation in your perspective. Without the hindrance of an unforgiven situation, you can move on to praying about new happiness. Forgiveness builds spiritual strength and enables the heart to endure misfortune or hardship, and to be a blessing to others.

A PRAYER PATTERN

☐ Find a quiet moment to sit down and think about the items that are troubling you.

☐ Write them down on a note pad. Some of them will look trivial and the moment you see them in black and white you will know they can be forgotten. Others may loom so large that you wonder why you have not already set out to correct them.

☐ First see the problem, and then act, by making forgiveness a daily part of your prayer life.

Father, You have forgiven us our sins.
Help us to be generous to others.
Take away the hidden sins
    which hinder us and cripple us
    in our daily walk with others.
Enable us to overlook obvious slights,
    and be oblivious to the frustrations
    which hinder our progress.
Wash out the stains of the past,
    and give us a clean slate on which to print
    happy words of the future
    in restored friendships
    and greater service.
                    Amen.

9/The prayer rug or kneeling pillow

One of the oldest religious customs in the world involves the use of prayer rugs or kneeling pillows. Tourists in foreign lands are often intrigued by their intrinsic beauty as well as by seeing how the lovely patterns fit into daily use by their owners.

Often a prayer rug is the last thing from which a religious pilgrim would part. For the pilgrim believes that the rug has a sacred connotation, and that contact can be made with God through kneeling upon the rug.

It is interesting to observe the many designs of such rugs, including those made by the North American Indians of the Southwestern desert. Sometimes an Indian woman will sit in the out of doors near a flowering cactus or close to a mountain, slowly putting a religious design into place as tourists watch.

The berries and grasses of the area are used for the tinting of the bland-colored hemp, so that the figures may appear in brilliant shades of red, purple, orange, or green, with a background of grey and brown or black.

Sometimes in travel I have been tempted to buy such a rug and bring it home as a reminder to me to always have my own place of prayer. Yet I have hesitated, even though I hoped to establish a solid habit of prayer.

Then one morning in a beautiful cathedral in England, I saw the craft of the parish women in designing pew pillows and kneeling cushions. A dedicated woman had organized the parish women into a needlework band, and each had made at least one pew pillow, adding her initials modestly in the corner.

The bright blues, roses and lavenders had faded into lighter shades as the yarn had seen daily use by those who came into the pews. The initials "CA" or "LH" meant nothing to the tourists, and perhaps not even to those who now remained in the village.

Yet the lovely handwork was a joy to behold. On a background of tiny needlepoint stitches someone had placed lovely patterns—a large cross, or a crown, a white lily or a red rose.

Infinite were the designs of beauty from hands now folded in death. A book could be purchased explaining the symbolism, but even this was not necessary to add to the loveliness of the moment. Something of the women themselves remained in the beautiful pillows, often used as miniature kneeling rugs.

Looking at a delicate daffodil design, I knew that

the time had come for me to make for myself a kneeling pillow. Back home, I searched through needlecraft books to find a pattern that spoke to my heart, even as the earlier lovely designs had appealed to the worshipping women in England.

Happily I sent away for the pattern book. When it arrived, the design looked so intricate and time-consuming that at first I hesitated to start. But a friend showed me where to insert the needle for the first stitch, and I began the plainest, simplest border.

Next came a contrasting color, easy to see, outlining the first flower in the nosegay. Soon I could see the shade that would automatically come next if I were to pick the flowers from my garden. Gradually the pillow grew in its beauty.

This did not happen overnight, but took a long time to fulfill. While I worked on it there was a matter of deep concern about which I was in prayer. Just seeing the pillow reminded me that it was time to pray about the pending decision.

At last the day came when the pillow was finished, stuffed and blocked. The first time I placed it on the floor in my writing room where I had been in the habit of kneeling on the carpet, the pillow felt soft but almost uncomfortable to my knees.

It soon took on the contour of my kneeling position, and now is almost a part of my body. When not in use, it stays tucked between the little white bookcase which is my temporary altar and the larger bookcase beside it. Out comes the pillow when there is a special matter for which I need to pray.

The fact that I have made the pillow with my own

hands somehow gives meaning to its use. For heart and hands must work together in this world to bring the answers to our prayers. Often even as we ask God to grant the answer, He can show us what we ourselves can do to help bring a better situation into being.

Since my own prayer pillow has come to have such meaning in my life, I have found it rewarding to make others for children. One little girl who lives in Yorkshire, England, half a world away from my California home, calls her rug her "praytime story rug." She runs to get it each evening and lies on it while her family reads a story, and then she turns and wiggles until she is on her knees, and uses it while she says her prayers. The rug I made for her is not of delicate needlepoint, but knitted of heavy yarn that is machine-washable. The variegated strands of pink and rose blend into a deep red, so it looks like a giant flower.

As the child uses the rug, she is forming the habit of prayer and is following one of the oldest customs in the world. Many ancient customs still have meaning for the space age, when adapted to our changing products and processes. New yarns and fabrics lend themselves to items as old in tradition as prayer rugs or kneeling pillows. Their use can be an inducement to current prayers about modern needs with thanks for daily blessings.

A PRAYER PATTERN————————————

☐ Find the most convenient place for you to kneel in prayer. This is in keeping with the Scripture, "But thou, when thou prayest, enter into thy closet, and when thou hast shut thy door, pray to thy Father which is in secret; and thy Father which seeth in secret shall reward thee openly" (Matthew 6:6).

☐ Consider making a prayer pillow or rug which can constitute your own "closet" or privacy in these days of crowded living quarters.

> *Dear Father, I come to this place of prayer*
> *asking for Thy companionship*
> *in a special way.*
> *In the privacy and silence of this moment,*
> *come into my heart*
> *with a new measure of Thy grace.*
> *Grant me courage*
> *to face today's problems*
> *whether large or small.*
> *Make me one with all the spiritual pilgrims*
> *who have prayed across the*
> *changing years.*
> *Let color and beauty be my companions*
> *in this earthly world*
> *which Thou hast made*
> *for all Thy children.*
> *Amen.*

10/Prayer classes

Some people derive great benefit from joining with others in prayer classes. Such groups remove the feeling of discouragement caused by loneliness, and often stimulate a prayer life which may have gone stale.

Prayer classes do not have to be large to be effective. One of the most helpful about which I have personal knowledge consisted at first of only two persons, soon enlarging to three. Without publicity the group began to grow as friends saw changes in the lives of those who were meeting for regular prayer sessions.

Soon, about 20 young mothers were meeting at a church social hall, with child care provided in the nearby nursery. It was my pleasure to speak to them one morning, and a more earnest group of truth seekers would be hard to find.

I recognized among them the young women who were the busiest workers in our community. They were the ones who rang doorbells for the Community Chest, acted as block leaders on the Cancer Crusade, and helped take the city-wide church census.

The woman in charge called the meeting to order and asked for special prayer requests. I was interested to see that some of the community activities were high on their list of priorities.

Yet the list also included many requests for more strength and courage with which to face individual problems. These included sickness in the home, a husband out of work, and a demanding mother-in-law who had recently moved into the home.

Honesty marked the session as the young women, who by now had established good rapport, made known their requests to each other as well as to God. It occurred to me that as each learned of the others' needs, there might be a growth of kindness and compassion when dealing with each other.

It is all too easy to sit at home alone and think that no one else has problems needing solution by prayer. When you take the first step toward joining a prayer class, you are automatically moving toward a greater understanding of the problems of others.

As I looked at these young women and thought how bravely they were shouldering their burdens in this time of inflation and breakdown in age-old family patterns, I recognized how important these two hours a week spent in group prayer were to them.

What they probably do not know at this point in their lives is that this time will produce many dividends in later years. For often, women who have met in such groups become such fast friends that the association lasts for many fruitful years. Friendships develop that help individuals bear the burdens of the changing years.

Psychology today testifies to the great importance of bringing our problems to the surface so that we can see exactly what is bothering us. Often we want the problem to change, or to go away and leave us alone. We did not ask for it, don't want it, and furthermore, don't see why we should have to figure out how to solve it.

The first thing to do is to rid ourselves of self-pity. In a prayer class, we are less apt to wallow in this self-pity than we are when alone. In fact, we may leave the prayer meeting seeing that in comparison with others and their problems, our own concern is small indeed.

Whenever this perspective occurs, it is a sign that the heart has been enlarged, and growth has been accomplished through prayer. Such growth comes when the problem is accepted for what it is, and not consigned to some fantasy land where we hope it will go into limbo and not bother us any more.

In one prayer class, I heard a young woman express it very well when she said, "I've decided that if I want this problem solved, I have to be the one to change. Nobody else is going to change apparently, so I have to start making the necessary changes in my own life."

She had grasped an essential and basic truth inherent in all powerful prayers: the breakthrough comes when an individual sees a personal, internal need for change and asks humbly for help in achieving it.

Sometimes a member of a prayer group can have a simple suggestion to make about how to start affecting that change. More often, the guidance may come when the individual is quietly waiting during a listening period in a prayer class.

Prayer classes also offer those attending a specific time for meeting to learn more about prayer. One of the chief handicaps to a successful prayer life at any age is the failure to set up a time pattern for such communion with God. But if it is known that a group will meet regularly and promptly on a Tuesday morning or a Wednesday evening, this helps keep prayer life constant. It provides encouragement if there is a definite date on the calendar when the distressed individual knows others also will be meeting for prayer help.

A word of caution is in order about attending such groups, for care must be taken that they do not ever become gossip sessions. Once the weaknesses of others are known, careful attention must be given to the tongue and lips so that confidences are not betrayed, adding further distress to those involved.

Spiritual strength comes also from linking the idealism of prayer classes with some action for good, such as collecting clothing for a family whose house recently burned, or planning meals for a family where the mother is hospitalized. A prayer class offers an opportunity to build energy for effective service.

A PRAYER PATTERN_____

☐ Look around you to see if there is a prayer group in your community in which you might fit and find spiritual help to grow in strength and grace.

☐ If there is none, and you feel the need of spiritual support through association with others, can you take this leadership? Invite two or three others to join you. The class will grow when positive results show in your own life.

Dear Heavenly Father, we thank Thee
    for the Bible promises of Thy help to us
    in all earthly circumstances.
Help us to believe them more fully
    and to realize them in our prayer lives
    as we try to change ourselves
    into better persons
    with Thy powerful help.
Grant us strength to move forward
    vigorously
    on the problems
    of our own church and community.
Keep our hearts and homes harmonious
    through the blessings that come
    through our prayer lives.
                Amen.

11/The telephone and prayer

When I wrote friends across the country about a physical problem and asked for their spiritual help, I was thinking in terms of receiving a letter back expressing their concern. Perhaps they would have a special verse of Scripture to suggest or words of counsel.

Instead, the telephone rang early one morning. Here was the voice of my friend. She said her husband was on their other telephone and would I please ask my husband to pick up the extension in his room.

She said forthrightly, "We want to pray with you, and right now. Why shouldn't we use the telephone as a gathering point since we can't be together in person?"

Obviously she was referring to the words of Jesus, who said in Matthew 18:20, "For where two or three are gathered together in my name, there am I in the midst of them."

The four of us held our telephone receivers while my friend's husband, who happens to be a minister, uttered a sincere prayer of thankfulness for past blessings and asked for help with the current situation. It was a moment when time and distance were completely forgotten. The connection was so clear that we seemed to be in the same room together.

This fellowship was so wonderful that it did seem there was a Presence with us. Something of that golden moment lingered with us during the difficult days that followed until the problem could be solved.

Why should it be thought unusual for a prayer to be given over the telephone? We live in the space age, and we need to take advantage of all possible new channels in meeting our spiritual demands as well as our material ones.

Prayer comes to us over television with the many church services that are broadcast on Sundays. On radio, prayer has long been a part of religious services. Some religious groups operate 24-hour prayer lines with easy-to-remember telephone numbers. Those in trouble can call at any hour of the day or night and be sure someone will be listening. This is the basis of many hot lines for suicide prevention, and for those involved with drugs.

If the telephone is so important in emergency matters, why should it not become a source of joyful use in prayer as well?

I was delighted when a young friend called the other day to say "Thank you for your prayers. The doctor is releasing my baby today, and I can take her home at noon." So I said to her that together we must thank God for this evidence of His goodness and for answered prayer. The telephone was the instrument by which we both praised God for what seemed to us a miracle in the recovery of the child.

There would be days ahead when this young mother would need to be encouraged in her efforts to care for her baby. She knew that her friends were as close as the telephone, and all she had to do was to pick it up and dial one of them for prayer.

Fortunately, we do not even have to dial when we wish to turn to God in prayer for any matter whatever. There is no central system to go through, no long number to remember, certainly no area code, for God is everywhere.

Prayer is a direct source of communication, and can be as simple as the reverent use of the one word "God." The three-word phrase "God help me" may be the most-used prayer in all the world. Usually it comes to mind immediately in difficult situations. Sometimes it is screamed in anguish, but in silent tones it is at the base of many prayers.

One of the ways God helps us is by showing us that there are others who will pray with us, if we contact them by note or telephone. In our own home, my husband and I felt an immediate surge of power when a friend with whom we have a close rapport undertook to add to his own busy schedule the matter of special prayer for a member of our family recovering from a serious illness. The bonds of our friendship were forged even stronger through such a great gift of loving and comforting prayer.

Sometimes we may be permitted even in our own weakness to make a similar gift to others. In fact, a possible solution to our own problem may be to pick up the telephone and call a shut-in to pass the time of day.

Sometimes those who have been most active in their business careers feel the most left out when they retire. This is particularly true of executives whose busy days have kept their lines ringing so often that they vowed they didn't even want a telephone when they retired.

One such man spoke to me over the telephone recently, and I was surprised to hear his voice, knowing his aversion to telephoning. "It took my illness to make me appreciate my telephone again," he confessed. He recently had had a pacemaker implanted to improve his heart condition, and he was currently prohibited from driving.

He said, "I've learned to like the telephone because it enables me to thank my friends for their kindnesses to me and my family during this difficult period. Will you and your husband promise to call me occasionally so I can hear your voices?" We were glad to restore this aspect of our friendship.

He had discovered that we are a part of each other in this life and that it helps to keep in touch. When your prayer life withers, try using new methods and mechanical means. Using the telephone together with prayer can produce happy fellowship and provide answers to problems of loneliness and the need for joint prayers of assurance.

A PRAYER PATTERN _____

☐ Take a new look at your telephone, and think of its possibilities for fellowship.

☐ Get out your address book and run down the list of names of those you promised faithfully you would call "someday." Can this be the "someday" you promised? Telephone rates are much lower over the weekends and holidays. It may surprise you to find how little it will cost to brighten the Sunday of some older friend who feels forgotten, or who needs special prayer.

*Father, we thank Thee for our
    instant communication with Thee
    through prayer.
Let us not limit ourselves
    to old-fashioned, rigid methods,
    but let our prayer circle be enlarged
    by the use of today's
    miracles of invention.
As we communicate with Thee,
    may we remember to keep in touch also
    with those who need Thy healing grace
    through a word of comfort
    and encouragement.
We ask believing in Thy name,
                    Amen.*

12/If we have
overlooked anything

Experience has shown us that prayers may seem to take wing and fly toward heaven. But sometimes, no matter how hard we pray, our prayers don't seem to get off the ground.

Then come the dragging days of seeming defeat when not only is the answer delayed, but the prayers themselves seem to have no zest and spirit, no matter how hard we try.

In all such instances I have been greatly encouraged by a most remarkable example of answered prayer observed one summer in Alaska. My husband and I had left our home in southern California to drive the Alaskan Highway to its farthest point, where the road runs out and stops.

We passed Anchorage and went on to Fairbanks, and were about to take the Steese Highway into

Circle City. We stopped for church that drizzly Sunday morning in a little church in Fairbanks.

I do not even remember what denomination it was, and by now the building has no doubt been replaced with a larger one, in keeping with the great expansion of the 49th state. All I remember is that the church was filled that morning, with many of the congregation talking in soft whispers as we entered.

In the front pews were a number of people, including children. Some women were wiping their eyes with handkerchiefs when the pastor stepped to the lectern to offer the morning prayer.

He prefaced it by saying that everyone surely knew the sorrow in the hearts of all the congregation. My husband and I listened carefully as he sketched the facts: one of their members had disappeared in his airplane that week, in company with two or three other men on a hunting trip.

Repeated searching had failed to uncover any trace of the downed plane, and almost all hope of finding the men alive was gone. The pastor thanked those in the congregation who had prayed with the family and provided companionship during the vigil.

Then he asked each member of the congregation to bow in silent prayer, concentrating on the men who were lost, and remembering especially the contribution that their friend had always made to the church and community. The pastor said he believed in the power of corporate prayer, and thought the congregation in its own silence could do more now than he could; he would bring the period to a close verbally after each prayer had been said in silence.

My husband and I added our prayers to the rest of the congregation and noted before bowing our heads that some of the lips were moving in silent conversation with God. After what seemed a very long time, the pastor cleared his throat and spoke. I shall always remember his moving words.

Even after a quarter of a century, I can hear the tenor of his voice in prayer: God, we have prayed all the prayers we know, and have done all we can think of in the way of a search for the lost. If we knew what else to do, we would do it. We come to Thee now in great humility. We ask Thee to please show us and tell us what it is *if we have overlooked anything.*

With that he stopped, apparently unable to go on in his emotion. There was a chorus of amens, and the brief church service continued. As we left the building and started on the rest of our journey, we kept thinking about the problem of the congregation and the sorrow that probably lay ahead for them.

So the next day we joined in the general rejoicing when we saw newspaper headlines announcing that the missing men had been found. Hastily we bought a paper to read with our dinner in the cafe. The story it told seemed almost incredible.

The rescuer said that he had been flying around on Sunday morning when he began to wonder *if he had overlooked anything.* On impulse he had turned at a very slight angle and gone to a more remote island, slightly off the search path. Flying low, he had seen the survivors waving to him. It had been comparatively simple to land and bring them home.

The words the pilot had used were almost an exact repetition of the very prayer given by the pastor and the congregation! It has become our watchword in difficult situations: "God, please tell and show us if we have overlooked anything."

It is surprising how often even the most obvious prayer overlooks some human element, which can be corrected by changing course. Perhaps it is a bad habit that can be changed into a good one. Maybe a course of action can be made better by kinder words or by curbing criticism.

When the way is kept open between man and God through humility, somehow the channels of prayer seem to flow more accurately and swiftly. The spiritual aim of each of us is to be rescued and not to have a feeling of being lost.

Often I remember the pilot who was able to rescue the stranded men because he had a feeling he might have overlooked something, and so changed course. Then I ask myself if I have taken time to sit down and think about the situation for which I am praying. Have I asked God to help me discover the apparent, which I may have been overlooking?

When I do this, light often shines on dark situations, leading to positive results. Maybe I need to make a telephone call to an expert, such as a lawyer, to get an answer to a problem that troubles me. What looms as a large problem to me may be a simple detail he can answer over the telephone from his expertise. Perhaps I need only to change my outlook from pessimism to cheerfulness in order not to overlook the important.

A PRAYER PATTERN

☐ List the known factors in the problem—lack of money, ill health, estrangement from a friend. Include the efforts that have been made to right the situation.

☐ Once these are known, take a good look at what else needs to be done to accomplish the desired end. Are you really sure you have followed the diet and exercise directions from your doctor? Could you telephone your friend with a luncheon invitation?

☐ When you ask God to show you what you may have overlooked in solving a problem, the answers do come!

> *Dear God, we would like to lead*
> *more effective lives,*
> *but sometimes we do not know how*
> *to accomplish our desires.*
> *We have tried*
> *and fallen short of our goal,*
> *and yet we do not wish to give up*
> *the dream.*
> *So we ask Thee to grant us*
> *special wisdom and insight*
> *to see what we have overlooked*
> *in our spiritual search.*
> *Stay with us on the journey.*
> *Grant us the power of Thy companionship.*
> *Amen.*

*". . .But in every thing by prayer and sup-
plication with thanksgiving let your requests be
made known unto God."*

Philippians 4:6

III/Types of Prayer

13/Material prayers

A woman said to me recently, "I wish I could believe in prayer as a way out of my problem." So I asked her if it were possible for her to define the problem, and if she wanted to tell me about it.

Was it an emotionally devastating problem concerning a loved one, such as a child's suspected use of drugs, or a husband's dependence on alcohol?

Was it worry over a family propensity to a disease for which there is at present no known cure? Or perhaps the recent death of a close relative?

To my surprise, it was none of these difficult situations that was bothering my acquaintance. She said life had become drab for her on a small income, and she felt her wardrobe was so shabby that she didn't want to go out any more, even to church.

I was so relieved to find her problem relatively

small that it took discipline to control a lighthearted response that might have discouraged her even more.

She asked me, "How could I possibly pray for better clothes? It seems so selfish and trivial, but I have to admit that this is at the base of many of my fears and problems."

As I searched for words that would not offend her pride, I told her that I was not sure how she could bring herself to do this unless she believed the promises of the Bible. Surely she remembered the words of Jesus about the lilies of the field.

The verses about their beauty are followed by a promise in Matthew 6:30: "Wherefore, if God so clothe the grass of the field, which today is, and tomorrow is cast into the oven, shall he not much more clothe you, O ye of little faith?"

I could understand my friend's reluctance to pray about clothes, but it was a joy to tell her that I pray material prayers, and that I believe there are answers to them. I shared with her an experience of my own involving clothes.

At the beginning of spring, I had placed my lackluster wardrobe of slacks and skirts on the bed and looked at it with little enthusiasm. "Blah" was the proper word, I told myself, for the shades of beiges and browns lying before me. I really needed some bright blouses to make the wardrobe seem new and give my spirits a lift.

Then reason reminded me that at today's inflated prices, it probably would be easier just to wear out these monotones. Budgeted money could instead be invested in one new bright outfit.

All during my morning period of meditation, the matter stuck in my mind. In keeping with my resolve to bring all things out into the open in prayer, I used words such as these: "God, I believe we were meant to look as nice as we can, all things considered, and that brightness sometimes helps to cheer a dull day. Then there is nothing wrong or hurtful in my wanting something better than these dull colors. How shall I go about getting the brightness without taking from others what they need or being overindulgent of self?"

That very noon on my way to shop for groceries, I stopped into a nearby department store to pick out a birthday card. To get to that section I had to walk by clothing racks, and my eyes saw a sign saying "Reduced." There hung three blouses—pink, blue, lavender. One was my size, the second marked a size smaller, and the third a size larger.

On impulse I held them up to the light and measured them, and found them identical in size. Someone had mismarked them at some point along the pricing line. All three would now cost less than the price of one that I had purchased earlier in the season.

Approaching a clerk, I showed her that all three measured alike in spite of the different sizes marked, and asked if she wanted to correct the marking for better sales. I also showed her the very low price tag, and asked if there were some mistake.

The girl smiled and said, "No, we have orders to clear out this merchandise before the end of the month. I'm just glad you can wear all three."

As she placed the three blouses in a box, first carefully wrapping each one in white tissue, she turned to me and said, "You have just shown me a pretty rainbow."

That is, in effect, what prayer does for us when we are willing to pray about such workaday things as a wardrobe: It is possible to find a rainbow.

If I had not taken the matter into my heart in my prayer period, I doubt very much that I would have been aware of the blouses on the reduced rack in my hurry to find a birthday card.

Prayer always heightens our awareness of needs and opportunities. I told my friend with her own clothing problem that perhaps if she tried prayer, she might be led not only to a solution for herself, but also to opportunities to serve others.

For on the same day on which I found my rainbow of blouses, I went straight home and took out three items to share with others. Most of us have items in our closets that can be shared with other men and women. Perhaps they are known to us personally, but if not, there are many opportunities to give to volunteer agencies, orphanages, or church and club rummage sales. When our own material prayers are answered, our thanks can be said best through sharing with others.

A PRAYER PATTERN _____

☐ Face honestly what it is that you really want to add to your happiness. Is it a colorful dress? A new rosebush for the garden? A bright skillet to hang over the stove? A new tool for the garage?

☐ If it is something that will make you happier and add to your effectiveness in working in your home or business, why isn't it right for you to have it? So why are you delaying? Commit the matter to prayer at this moment.

Dear Father, forgive me my unhappiness
    and restlessness
    and, above all, my procrastination
    in finding what I need
    to make life more beautiful.
Keep me aware
    of that which I need and want.
Help me
    to walk the pathways
    where these things will become
    available.
May I always both enjoy
    and share
    that which comes from Thy hand,
Even as I pray
    in Thy Generous Name,
    the Giver of perfect gifts.
        Amen.

14/Guidance is where you find it

A prayer offered frequently is the heart-felt one for guidance. Often this is the central plea of prayers given from church lecterns, at altars and in homes. On sleepless nights we toss and turn while we beseech God for guidance in some family problem that seemingly has no solution. But guidance is such an elusive concept, we wonder if we will recognize it when we finally receive it.

Sometimes we look backward and realize that we did have guidance at some specific time along the way, but were too dull-witted to recognize it for the divine help it might have provided.

This suggests that perhaps our minds are already made up and we do not really seek fresh guidance, but rather a reinforcement of a specific course of action we are already determined to pursue.

However, when we are sincere in truly seeking guidance, it often comes in unexpected ways. We must learn to attune ourselves to seeing it.

In my own life, a remarkable answer to prayer for guidance came at the doorway to a happy holiday party which I had attended in spite of a deep soreness in my heart. "How can I ever put on a long dress and a smile and go out to meet people tonight?" I had asked my husband at the end of a long solemn day of study about a serious situation.

But the friends were always cordial hosts, and my husband and I knew the feeling of friendship in their home would restore our dragging spirits. So reluctantly I dressed with some glitter for the occasion. At the party, I hoped I was giving the right responses in small talk with other party guests.

As we were leaving, the door opened and in walked two old friends whom we had not seen for a while. The wife greeted us cheerfully and her doctor-husband said to me, "I dropped into your mother's room at the hospital this afternoon while your father was visiting with her, so I had time with them both."

Instantly, I wondered if he had been called in on consultation. "No," he said, "I was waiting on that floor of the hospital, and I just went in to say hello to your parents."

His kindness expressed at the end of this puzzling day brought a quick tear to my eye as I tried to thank him for this thoughtful gesture during his busy day. He turned back and stepped outside the door under the stars and asked me what I was so worried about.

I found my words tumbling out: "Oh, if I only knew what to do! I've prayed all day for guidance. At nine o'clock tomorrow morning there is to be a hospital conference, and I have to decide whether Mother goes home and tries to use her walker, or goes into a convalescent home. The decision is absolutely driving me up the wall!"

He nodded, and I plunged ahead: "I want so much to do the right thing, but I can't figure out what it is. I'm torn between whether they can manage together in their own home, or whether she would be better off with professional care. How can I possibly 'play God' and separate people who have lived together for nearly 70 years of marriage? And yet not even the doctors are sure whether Mother can manage on her own since the stroke."

My friend waited in silence and then spoke slowly and deliberately: "In a long practice, I have discovered that you always have to take some risks for happiness in this life."

At his words, my heart gave a leap of recognition. Here, where I least expected to find it, was the guidance I had sought on my knees. Of course you have to take some risks in this life! We do it all the time for money, or in our careers—but how often do we do it for happiness' sake?

The answer was clear to me: I had to let my parents try to manage together at home no matter what the cost in energy. I had to face the risk of failure; if they could not manage, then other arrangements would have to be made, perhaps when strength was even less than now.

The next morning, we took my mother out of the hospital to her home. It was not easy to set up a schedule and keep to a routine, but it paid off in restored health and happiness and over three more years of companionship.

Guidance had come partly because we had managed to socialize in spite of problems, to go where there was the possibility of laughter and gaiety. We have learned that an important part of guidance is to keep moving, and not to sit at home alone brooding, while the mind churns around with the same old problems.

Guidance may seem to come in a chance remark, but who is to say that it is chance? If we believe in guidance through prayer, isn't it possible that we were intended to be at the door when the friend arrived with the answer? Even he did not know he had the answer, but was an instrument for delivering it. He was a part of the solution to the problem that I had offered to God in prayer, seeking guidance.

Sometimes we may be enabled to be a part of guidance from God in ways beyond our knowing, just through a smile, a handshake or a telephone call, because we are thinking hard about someone and feel we must follow through. If your prayers for guidance do not seem to be answered, look closely and listen well to those around you. God provides earthly guidance through others when we continue to ask and to look for solutions.

A PRAYER PATTERN

☐ Ask again for guidance about a career matter, an investment problem, or a health situation.

☐ In the stillness, resolve to recognize answers when they are presented. Then go about your daily routine with a lighter heart.

☐ Return to your place of meditation at evening and look back over the day's encounters. Has something happened to give you a fresh clue as to how to act? If not, there is always tomorrow. While you are asleep, your subconscious mind may work upon the material fed into it today in your routine, and may present you with an answer.

Dear God, forgive us our feverish
and frantic efforts
in trying to find answers.
Help us to become still enough to recognize
that in our own established routines
there are those who long to help,
even as we have helped them,
sometimes without our knowing.
Keep us aware of the needs of others,
and let them become a part
of the answers to our own quests
for truth.
We thank Thee that Thou
dost not leave us alone without guidance,
and that we may pray as we do now,
in Thy dear name.
                    Amen.

15/Praying for physical healing

One of today's most controversial prayer issues concerns prayers for physical healing. Sometimes when we pray unceasingly for the healing of a beloved person, prayers seem to go unanswered.

Sometimes, instead of physical recovery, death comes. The family mourns and may begin to doubt the effectiveness of prayer even though it has proven to be of comfort in past circumstances.

There are other instances when death would be preferred to long lingering and suffering. Yet the patient lives on, despite prayers asking either for healing or a blessed release.

All such instances emphasize again that the answers to prayers are in the hands of God and His infinite wisdom. Some whose prayers go completely unanswered turn from God and lose all faith in healing prayer. Others keep on praying on the premise that lifting others into the light of God's healing love is the most helpful way to try to solve all aspects of the problem of family illness. For when a loved one is ill, many other difficulties usually arise, ranging from finances to housing or nursing care.

All such circumstances involve the matter of finding the right time to voice prayers for physical healing. One of the most successful prayers I know is a woman well advanced in years, to whom friends turn automatically with problems of healing.

She does not claim to have special power, but she does keep her word when she promises to deal with a matter through prayer. She confided to me, in a time of fellowship, the secret of her prayers for healing. She said, "I use the time I spend on my own body in praying for the bodies of others." She explained that she had come to this decision because she could not find other time due to her own physical infirmities.

"I have to spend much time in the bathtub, letting my limbs soak, and allowing hot water to give me relief from my own pain. So, many years ago I decided to use this time in prayer for the physical relief of those who had asked me for healing prayers."

With her own body stretched out in the water, she is reminded of her friends who are in trouble physically.

"If it is a broken arm that has not mended properly, I put the washcloth on my own arm while I pray for the relief of the symptoms of my friend," she told me with charming innocence.

On a recent summer holiday, she recalled, a young boy had caught his foot in his bicycle and was filled with both pain and fright as they took him to the doctor. "I concentrated on my own foot, realizing how intricately it is made, while I prayed for the skill of the doctors in repairing the foot of my young friend."

The little boy made a remarkable recovery, as did the friend with the injured arm. None of us can know how much help came from the specific prayers of my praying friend, but her case is an example of one means that can be used in lifting our loved ones into the light of God's healing love. Isn't it advantageous to take every opportunity to link the body and prayer when asking for healing?

Because she handles her own physical difficulties so well, I believe that my friend has truly discovered a secret that might work for others. When I have tried it for myself, the system has had two visible effects.

First, it lets my friends know I am cognizant of their needs when I promise to pray for their physical healing. And, in some subtle way it makes me more appreciative of my own functioning body and often relaxes it.

This was proven on a morning when I received an urgent telephone call from a friend who was in a hospital undergoing tests for undiagnosed stomach pains. Lying in my morning tub, I placed a hot towel across my middle. As I prayed for my friend's relief from pain, some of my own hidden tensions faded away. My stomach muscles became much more relaxed than they had been for some time.

Such prayers as these can be done in complete privacy. The only sound is that of the water gushing from a shower or flowing into a tub. In rare privacy, surrounded by the silence of isolation, the mind and heart can be tuned to important physical problems while some of the trivia of the day recede.

Thrown back upon our own resources, we see again our common humanity and our mutual need for dependence upon God, the Giver of life. Even more, reverence for the body may be increased.

The Bible says in John 2:21, in referring to Jesus, "But he spake of the temple of his body." If the body indeed is to be considered as a temple, then we may with confidence use our bodies to emphasize our ministry through prayer.

Even as the temple in Jesus' day had to be cleansed from the worldly activities that defiled it, so our own bodies may need to be cared for more tenderly if they are to engage in a ministry of prayer. Health truly falls within the category of one of God's greatest gifts to His children. Whatever the evil appearance of injury or illness may be at this moment, restored health can be made a matter of earnest prayer leading to healing.

A PRAYER PATTERN _____

☐ Reflect on the wonder of your own body. Remember all the miles your feet carry you within a day, a week, a month, a year.

☐ Think of the needs of those you love. Ask with an air of expectation that those in need may be healed of their infirmities.

☐ End with a prayer of thanksgiving for all the normal body functions that we often take for granted.

> *Dear God, hear our prayers for healing.*
> *We lift our bodies*
>   *into the light of Thy healing love,*
>   *and ask for Thy blessing*
>   *on us and on our bodies.*
> *Help us to use energy wisely*
>   *day by day*
>   *so that our strength may be*
>   *directed to positive areas*
>   *of influence.*
> *Forgive us for poor physical habits.*
> *Keep us active and healthy*
>   *in our service to others,*
>   *as we pray now in Thy name,*
>   *Amen.*

16/The "almost there" prayer

One of the most frustrating prayer problems is the feeling that if we could only get a little further along, we could know the answer for sure. I call this situation the "almost there" prayer.

On one occasion I received such a wonderful answer that I try now to continue praying until the new frustration is overcome. The outstanding answer to my "almost there" prayer occurred in Japan.

Before we left home on our round-the-world trip, our pastor had handed my husband and me the address of our church missionaries, who had served for 40 years in Japan in a rural area outside the port city of Kobe. We did not know them except as names in our church bulletin and as the people to whom we had sent money to help buy a station wagon for use in their work.

Furthermore, we did not expect to have time to look them up, but it so happened that our ship had an extra day in port in Kobe. So I pulled out our address book and said, "Why don't we find these people and deliver in person the assorted greetings we've been given for them by our friends at home?"

My husband agreed, and we went by taxi to the railroad station. There we were told by an English-speaking clerk that the train was not running because of a one-day strike. We started to accept this as defeat, but learned that there were electric cars that went that way from another section of town.

By now I was ready to go back to the ship and read a book, but my husband enjoys a good travel challenge. So we set out to find the other station, and once there, inquired again how to get to the little town.

Eventually a young man interceded for us, saying he had learned his English from GIs and was glad to have a chance to help. He told us that it would take us most of the afternoon to get out there, and then we would have to take a taxi from the station, but he thought some vehicle would be available.

So we climbed into the electric car. It was much like our own streetcars, and we enjoyed watching the passengers climb aboard in kimonos or western garb. I remember three women who scrambled aboard at the first stop carrying huge sacks of grain. A man nearby volunteered to tell us when we were approaching our stop, having noted we were Americans. He wanted to tell us about his year at a school in the Midwest, so time passed pleasantly.

When we stepped off the car and onto the little sidewalk by the depot my heart sank, for this was indeed out in the country. Eventually a broken-down automobile appeared with a friendly Japanese cab driver who did not know one word of English. All we could tell him was the name of the town, which proved to be something like a little district.

He looked at the directions written on the paper in my hand, but he could not understand the Japanese words written by the man in the station. He did recognize the one word for the village, and set out lickety-split to take us there. When we arrived, there was no one we could ask for directions.

I remember looking out of the auto, now stopped at the main street, and seeing the pink petals of the cherry blossoms against a darkening sky and wondering why I had ever chosen to spend this Sunday afternoon of my life in this manner.

By now my husband was also ready to return to Kobe, for all efforts of the cab driver to find someone who could read the directions seemed futile. In desperation, I climbed out of the car and asked the men to remain there while I walked down the road to look at a little garden where blue and white iris had tempted me as we passed.

Walking down the road I prayed my very first "almost there" prayer. It went something like this: "Dear God, we are a long way from home—California to Japan. Somewhere within a block or two are people from our hometown who have not seen anyone from there in years. It seems to us to be right and good that we should get together this Sunday, but we cannot do it unless You will somehow show us the way." Then I just stood still and looked at the flowers.

I was about to turn to hike back to the car when I suddenly knew which way to go to reach the home of the missionaries. I felt I should walk up a nearby hill. Aloud I said, "Amen and thank You," and walked back to the car. I asked my husband and the taxi driver to follow me.

My husband thought I was slightly crazy, but reluctantly joined me. We climbed a little hill near a playground, and at the top saw a short street with three houses. I went to the middle house and pulled the string of the little tinkling bell by the doorway.

Wondering whether it would be opened by a Japanese or an American, I waited in suspense. The door opened and there stood the woman whose picture I had seen in our church bulletin. I gave her my name and hometown and she promptly burst into tears and hugged me.

"You are the first members of our church who have ever visited us in these 40 years," she said. "Time and again I have cleaned house and laid in food, and always travelers have thought it was too much trouble or they had too little time to take the train to our village. I can't believe this wonderful surprise—and I don't know how you ever did it, because the trains are on strike today."

We went indoors for a wonderful heartwarming visit. It seemed that each Sunday evening they had kept the tradition of dining on waffles with syrup and canned butter, a supper they had enjoyed at home as young people in the United States. We joined them, and later they took us in the church station wagon back to the last electric car to Kobe.

Years later, when these missionaries retired to our hometown, they never tired of telling of their one visit by fellow church members made possible by my first "almost there" prayer. We shared a wonderful friendship in their last years and attended their golden wedding anniversary party. Their friendship reinforced our belief in the "almost there" prayer.

A PRAYER PATTERN ────────────────────

☐ Think of the matter on which you despair at the moment, but which seems to you to be right and good. Is it the right vocation for a young person? Is it knowing how to make your own will and facing up to your death?

☐ In many ways we are "almost there," but never quite willing or ready to make the right decision. Ask God to take you the rest of the way when you have gone as far as you can in your own wisdom.

> *God, we are so grateful*
> > *that we can rely on Thee for answers*
> > *when our own finite will fails us.*
> *Keep us from deep discouragement*
> > *which comes from feeling*
> > *that we must give up*
> > *and turn back.*
> *Help us to hold on just a little longer*
> > *until we can see the problem clearly*
> > *and know that Thou wilt guide us*
> > *to the right ending.*
> *Keep us from being lost in a maze*
> > *in life's journey,*
> > *and bring us to our rightful place*
> > *in Thy Kingdom,*
> > *through Thy name,*
> > > *Amen.*

17/Prayers of hands and heart

When the telephone rang one after-noon, I had just settled down in a chair with a good book, determined to keep cool on a hot day. The caller changed all that, for she said in a choked voice:

"My husband is undergoing emergency surgery right now in an attempt to save his life, and I need you to pray for him."

So, saying goodbye to a quiet afternoon, I put aside my book, went to my place of prayer, and got down on my kneeling pillow.

I prayed for a long time—and listened for guid-ance—before I got to my feet again. I knew I could not return to the chair and the book. What more could I do this afternoon to be of spiritual help to my friends? Should I try to telephone others, asking for their help?

No, it was prayer she had asked for, and my heart was filled with it. But what about my hands? It was then that God gave me guidance that has proved tremendously useful in many situations since.

In a moment of vision, I realized that what my hands needed was some sort of repetition, whereby each time I went through a specific motion, I could treat it as a prayer to God to sustain my friends in this crisis.

One of the things that came to my mind was the task of putting address labels on envelopes, a time-consuming chore that I do not enjoy, but which must be done.

With a stack of envelopes on a table to my left, the return address stickers to my right, and a small moistened sponge in between, I began the repetitious task with my hands, thus freeing my mind completely for prayer.

How wonderfully sweet was that hour of spiritual fellowship, spent linked to God and my friends in mind and heart while my hands performed this routine task. Before I knew it, the work was done, and in my heart I had a feeling of relief as though the surgeons also had been able to do their work well. All of us had been lifted up to the healing light of God, through heart and hands in unison.

How well this worked was brought home to my husband and me vividly one day the next spring when, in answer to the ring of the doorbell, we found the same couple standing at our doorway. The wife, who had telephoned me earlier, was smiling broadly, and her husband held in his hands a beautiful Easter lily with seven blossoms.

As he entered our hallway, he turned to my husband and me and said, "I promised myself in the hospital months ago that as soon as I could drive again, the first place I would come would be to your home to say thank you for your prayers."

For a moment I could not speak. I put the plant on the hall table, where its flowers remained in beautiful array for over a month. Later, my husband planted the lily in our garden.

Never before had we had any luck in encouraging Easter lilies to grow outside in our yard, but this one seems to know it carries a special story of love as well as beauty, for the plant blossoms profusely year after year.

Whenever we see its lovely delicate blooms we are reminded of the intimate moment when the wife called for help, and the blessed day when her recovered husband came to speak his thanks.

In between there had been many more prayers, the sending of some cards and some telephone calls of encouragement. But most of the praying had been done while working at chores of repetitious monotony, made new by the knowledge that they could be dedicated to prayer.

From this experience and many others, we discovered that when hands and heart work together in prayer, the prayers seem to be most helpful. They carry with them comfort to the one who receives, and also help the one who gives by transferring emotion into action.

I recall the busy career woman who came to my

doorway with a freshly baked peach cobbler at a time of serious illness in our family. She was on her way to pick up her children at the playground and she had no time to step into my house.

She had put the cobbler into the oven the minute she got home from work, while she was making her own supper plans. "I wanted you to know I was thinking of you and that we have you in our prayers," she told me. "My little girl thinks so much of your mother, and she added her name as 'Grammy P' at the end of her prayers for our own family last night."

How much this simple expression of faith and concern warmed my heart! It seemed that the cobbler tasted especially good, and perhaps it did, for the best ingredient of family baking is love for those who will partake of it.

Needlework and handicraft activities also provide opportunities for loving service through prayer, using hands and heart together. I remember that my grandmother would pick up a spool of pink crochet thread and start making tatting loops. Soon all of us grandchildren would have handkerchiefs with lovely pink tatting when our birthdays arrived.

Sometimes I would see her lips move as she worked, and I know now that she was offering up prayers for our lives and for our success in our schoolwork. For how she rejoiced when we had good news to bring her, and how she enjoyed going to school programs.

Today, even though I do not keep up the tradition of such needlework, one of my cherished possessions is her sterling silver tatting shuttle. As I look at its shiny brightness in my needlework box, I remember Grandma with her swiftly moving fingers, and her ceaseless prayers for our happiness.

In any home, there is no lack of opportunity for setting up the prayer-of-repetition routine. Since I have done so, life's daily tasks have given new meaning and pleasure to my years. When you are faced with an emergency, or bogged down in depressing details, why not try to find renewed energy through using prayers of hands and heart?

If we can learn to make our chores a part of our prayer life, we may be able to accomplish much more with less stress. Our bodies will relax and our minds will become freer to think of others who are bravely carrying their own burdens. We will have taken a step toward a spiritually oriented life of service.

A PRAYER PATTERN ————————————

☐ Select your most monotonous housekeeping chore. Think about it in a new way by asking yourself some questions. Is there a way you can do it in a shorter amount of time? Can you sit instead of stand? Make yourself physically comfortable, and then release your energy in prayer.

☐ Resolve to combine hands and heart in offering comfort to others by integrating prayer with something made in your kitchen or hobby shop. Think of what you are making with your hands as the tangible part of your intangible prayers for those whose burdens are a part of your own concern.

> *Dear God, we feel so helpless*
> *to really show our sympathy*
> *in many instances of life.*
> *But with the help of both hands and heart,*
> *we hope to make our grieving friends*
> *understand that*
> *we do care.*
> *Above all, we would like to give*
> *the reassurance of Thy great*
> *loving concern*
> *in all human areas of living.*
> *Help us to make the right gesture*
> *in the right way*
> *to Thy honor and glory,*
> *as we pray in Thy dear name,*
> *Amen.*

18/The prayer of intercession

One of the joys of growing into an active prayer life comes when the heart learns the power of intercessory prayer.

Intercessory prayer involves another person, and means that the heart is turned outward from personal problems, at least for the moment of praying for the other person. This may call for the choosing of a prayer partner to whom one may turn instantly for extra-special help when a matter zooms into importance on the prayer horizon.

One elderly friend who is now confined to bed in a rest home is known as a real warrior in prayer battles. Another friend expressed it well when he said, "I sure like having her on my side when it is a matter of praying for the outcome of some project calling for lots of strength."

Why is this friend so powerful in her prayer life?

It is because she recognizes positive factors and casts away all negative doubts. She thinks of intercessory prayer as an active factor, not a passive one of "just praying."

Too often our prayers seem to go round and round in circles and to come back to the same starting point. We wonder whether they have risen off the ground. It is not ours to wonder, but to stay faithfully and prayerfully in the attitude of intercession.

Sometimes the person for whom prayer is being offered may feel he does not even wish prayer. But who can know what power is released in praying for others? Perhaps this very act of intercession will enable the person eventually to open his heart to the healing blessings of prayer. Seeming miracles have been known to occur long after the time when the original prayers of intercession were offered.

It is as though there were a great deep well in the Garden of Prayer into which requests can be placed. It may seem at times as though the prayers are being dropped endlessly into the well. Then again the answers seem to begin to rise to the top.

Why should this be? Can it be that, as we pray, the love in our own hearts expands and becomes the substance that lifts our prayers from the bottom of life's well into the present with opportunities for positive action? When intercessory prayers are undergirded with love, they often bring loving results.

Intercession through prayer takes time, and this is why it is sometimes overlooked as an energizing factor in life. Yet those with even limited strength can use their time in prayer for others. The strange thing is that sometimes those who are ill begin to show the most improvement when they begin to pray for others.

Intercession always involves both patience and persistence. Sometimes the one for whom the prayers are being said seems to lack any form of gratitude. That person may even scoff at the one who continues to pray.

This is particularly true of young people who in trying their own wings turn away from parents who have believed in lifting Godward on wings of prayer. Yet recently a young man said to me shyly, "I'm so glad you and my folks kept on praying for me during all my trouble."

He had found a young woman companion who understood his sometimes tempestuous moods, and who had stability enough to keep him on the forward path. She served as a bridge between his own youthful impetuosity and the solidarity of his parents. Once more it was a joy to be in that home.

The mother said to me, "What would we have done without the intercession of friends in their prayers for our son?" For the family had reached the point where it could not pray without being torn apart with tears and reproaches.

All of us need to spend some time in intercessory prayer for others. In this uncertain life, we never know when we ourselves may suddenly stand in need of the intercession of others on our behalf, or for those whom we love and hold dear.

What if we need to have our own faith replenished through the prayers of others? Then confess this fact to a friend and say, "Please take over for me in this prayer matter." Do not be ashamed to admit weakness and ask help from others.

The important factor is to remember to keep lifting the one in need of help so that this person is brought through prayer into the light of God's healing love. There, health and strength can come to rest on the weakened or ill or discouraged person.

Intercession carries the individual into the realm of God where He alone has power to heal, working sometimes through physicians or psychiatrists, or perhaps through loving friends.

One means of intercession is simply to repeat such a phrase as "God bless John," using the Christian given name. Such prayers can be given while at work, around the house, or on waking in the middle of the night.

Intercession involves thinking of others, and putting behind us the selfish prayers that are so often heard, such as "Give me, God," and "Grant me, God," and "Remember me, God."

Even the person most practiced in prayer needs to stop once in a while to see if intercessory prayer is a part of the spiritual routine. For always, intercessory prayer leads from selfishness to a wider circle of usefulness. It can cause us to grow in grace through the changing years, and can remain with us as a blessing to the end of life.

A PRAYER PATTERN _____

☐ Consider well whether you are in need of a prayer partner to help you intercede in behalf of some loved one who faces a real problem. In my life for many years it was a friend in a rest home. Through daily prayer she gave me spiritual support to undertake many things that she could no longer do for herself.

☐ Can you make a compact with some friend to engage in mutual intercessory prayer in behalf of a personal problem or some group project?

> *God, we ask Thee to intercede*
> > *on behalf of those we love,*
> > *and for those who stand*
> > *urgently in need of Thy help.*
>
> *We remember the precious Scripture that*
> > *tells us of Thy power:*
> > *(Ephesians 3:20, 21) "Now unto him that is*
> > *able to do exceeding abundantly above*
> > *all that we ask or think, according to*
> > *the power that worketh in us,*
> > *Unto him be glory. . . ."*
>
> *We believe we can touch this power*
> > *through prayer,*
> > *and we ask Thee now to help all*
> > *who lack strength and peace of mind.*
>
> *We pray in Thy dear name,*
> > > *Amen.*

19/The prayer
of humility

One of the treasures in my writing room is a little black metal plaque bearing the words of a famous old prayer attributed to fishermen: "Dear God, be good to me; the sea is so wide, and my boat is so small."

I treasure this keepsake for its precious words of humility and because it was given to me by a cherished friend at the end of a happy afternoon at the seashore.

We had made a trip to visit a mutual friend who lives near the ocean, and had gone shopping after a leisurely luncheon. When we returned home at sunset, my friend took from her bag a little package that I had noticed a clerk wrapping for her while I browsed the bookstands.

"We have had such a good day together, and you have been such a loyal prayer partner to me for so long," she said. "I want you to have this, with love from me."

The beauty of that moment of giving has never left me, and often I pray the same words as do the fishermen, for all of us sooner or later have reason to know what that prayer means. The words express mankind's humility in seeking the help of the God of the universe whose sea is so great.

We feel small indeed, for things happen to damage the confidence we have had in our own ability to cope with life. Perhaps we lose our job, or our child requires expensive medical treatment, or there are retirement problems. We know at such times that our human boat is so small.

Fortunate is the heart which knows that while the sea is wide, it is possible to approach the God of the sea and ask Him to be "good to me." When we become humble in our seeking, God, in His goodness, will loose His blessings into the home and heart of the one who asks.

Often we are like the child who feels no help is necessary in putting on shoes and stockings, but who tries to put the left shoe on the right foot. Recently I watched the grandchild of a friend struggle and struggle until tears came, because she refused to let anyone help her put on her shoes. The grandmother remained firm that the child must first ask for the help.

Finally the little girl turned to me with tears running down her cheeks and held out her hands to me, and then pointed to her shoes. The grandmother smiled to me and nodded, so I untangled the shoestrings to help the child, and enjoyed her contented sigh when the shoes were on straight. Why should we, as adults, feel we also can ask strangers for help more easily than we can ask God? For, as we read in James 1:17: "Every good gift and every perfect gift is from above, and cometh down from the Father of lights, with whom is no variableness, neither shadow of turning."

Is our reluctance because of our pride? We don't want to be bothered with prayer on good days, and we have too much pride to ask in time of need. In our personal relationships, we don't like to be taken for granted when things are going smoothly and then be turned to in times of distress. Such actions prove to be destructive in friendships.

But this is often how we act in our relationship with God. It takes something grave to cause us to put aside our pride and kneel in prayer. The first reaction is apt to be excuses as to why we have not prayed earlier:

"I was too busy, God; You know how hard it has been to keep up payments on the house, and how long I've worked overtime to get the necessary money. I really haven't had time to pray until now. And all the worry over inflation and maybe losing the house has me scared stiff."

A first step comes when we realize the excuses can be put aside. All we really need to do is to ask in deep humility: "Dear God, be good to me."

When we are willing to admit that we need God to be good to us, it becomes easier to see that we also need family and friends to be good to us if our way is to become easier in the future. And this in itself implies that we must first learn to be good to those with whom we come in daily contact.

Recognizing that "the sea is so wide" shows us how vast are the problems that confront our fellow human beings in the daily tasks of earning a living, keeping within a budget and trying to preserve sufficient health and energy for community activities.

Finally, the recognition that our own "boat is so small" puts the situation into proper perspective. We may have magnified our personal problems out of all proportion. Maybe all we need is to realize that they are small enough for us to handle—with the ever-present help of God.

The long-term illness can be broken down into months, weeks, days, and then into hours. Perhaps some help can be found for just one portion of a large problem, making it manageable.

If we are willing to accept small gifts, and if we use them as they come, we become prepared for greater gifts. As we become aware of what is available in larger portions, our hearts enlarge to receive more of God's loving blessings.

Without humility, we want the whole answer, and we want it right now. With humility, we are able to accept the little help available, and use it wisely as a basis on which to build toward the final solution. Whenever I glance at the plaque that my friend presented as a love gift, I feel great humility for the blessing of human friendship, as well as for the loving companionship God offers His children through the avenue of prayer.

A PRAYER PATTERN ———————————————

☐ Face realistically your most pressing current problem. Try to see if pride is keeping you from a direct prayer asking for help.

☐ If so, confess this pride now, just to yourself and to God. No one else has to know what is in your heart, and God already knows.

☐ Relax and know the joy of true humility. Accept the lighter load when pride goes from your heart, and the burden from your shoulders.

> *Dear God, we are all like fishermen,*
> *   and their prayer speaks for us.*
> *We do not have to find fresh words*
> *   to ask for Thy help.*
> *We thank Thee*
> *   for the vastness of the world,*
> *   and for the fact that we may share*
> *   in it.*
> *Please accept our thanks*
> *   for Thy goodness to us,*
> *   and help us to reflect that goodness*
> *   in humble daily living.*
> *   Amen.*

20/The prayer
that won't go away

No matter how many wonderful answers to prayers we may receive in this life, there is usually one prayer that won't go away, and which remains unanswered, sometimes for years.

This haunting unanswered prayer often causes deep resentment and bitterness in the heart of the one who prays it because there seems to be no evidence of an answer. At the least, the unanswered prayer may seem embarrassing or humiliating when family and friends know of your prayers.

No one likes the prayer that won't go away. Yet this prayer often is a powerful force for good in building character through an active, persistent prayer life. It can help develop a powerful faith that is a witness to others.

Maybe it is a wife who keeps praying that her

husband will be able to overcome his weakness toward liquor. Meanwhile, she becomes more gentle and at the same time stronger in her own approach to living through the comfort of the prayer.

A devoted husband and father may grieve because his wife is so discontented that family harmony seems impossible. He sees his children becoming confused and restless, and longs to have his prayers for harmony answered. While he gives his children companionship, he continues to pray the prayer that won't go away.

Then again, the prayer that won't go away may be a prayer to overcome a fear. A lonely person fears making new friends, because earlier friends have disappointed. As present friends disappear in this mobile society, it becomes even harder to keep on trying to build a circle of friendship. A continued prayer for the ability to learn friendliness can provide support in a difficult situation.

Offices of counselors are filled with people who become discouraged over their own secret prayers that won't go away, and which do not come to a solution. In such times in my own life I have often comforted myself with the philosophy of a gardener friend who plants many bulbs each year and who once told me, "You have to plant prayers deep, too."

He meant that you have to dig deep enough into the soil of life to be sure that your prayers are reaching down where they might find spiritual moisture and nourishment. You shouldn't just offer a prayer and go off and leave the matter; you must keep on with your spiritual "digging." If you stop too soon, the prayers might prove to be as rootless as our gladioli garden was one year.

I had been given some rare new bulbs by a friend who knows how much I enjoy the new varieties, some as lovely as lavender orchids or as frilly as white petunias. In a great hurry to get them into the ground because rain was beginning to fall, I dug only shallow holes. When the gladioli grew tall, they flopped over to the ground and the beautiful flowers were covered with dust. Their beauty was spoiled because I had been in too much of a hurry to keep digging into the soil for a firm foundation.

Remembering this, I tried to keep on praying about my own prayer that would not go away. On the scale of importance of prayers, mine did not rank very high, and some of my closest friends did not even understand why I needed to make my fear a matter of prayer.

They dismissed my fear as unworthy of one who believes that God is in charge of the universe, which includes sky, sea and earth, the stars, moon and sun. The sad truth is that I was afraid to fly.

This does not mean that I did not get into airplanes and did not take trips. Indeed, before my fear of flying could be taken away, I had flown the equivalent of twice around the world. But any trip meant I would have white knuckles, tense stomach muscles and a tightened throat. Not for me the window seat—I didn't care what was on the ground beneath me. The most I could manage was to enjoy the passing clouds.

I recall one beautiful night when my husband and

I were flying over the polar route to England, and
the rest of the plane was filled with sleeping passengers. The pilot strolled through in a relaxed fashion
and said, "You seem to be the only person awake.
I'm glad somebody is enjoying this beautiful night
with me."

I nodded, too scared to open my mouth and speak
to him. Grimly I forced myself to endure flying, all
the time knowing that God had put the sky here for
His children to enjoy with Him and with each other.
And I kept on praying the prayer that would not go
away—"Please give me release from this terrible
fear."

My prayer did not seem to rise toward heaven, and
it wouldn't leave me. Then one day, in one magic
moment, all the years of fear vanished in an experience so beautiful it was breathtaking and will be
with me each day for the rest of my life.

We were en route from Denmark on a flight from
Copenhagen to Los Angeles. My husband was ill, and
to make him more comfortable I had given up my
aisle seat. As I sat by the window, I looked fearfully
down onto snow and ice.

Suddenly a town emerged. I could see the roofs of
stores, schools, and houses and the steeples of
churches. In the sunlight, the brilliant icicles sparkled like jewels. I wondered why the streets looked
so dark until it occurred to me that I must be seeing
frozen water, and that these could be canals in Holland.

Just then the pilot announced, "Below is the most
beautiful view of the city of Amsterdam I have ever

seen on this route." It was a perfect picture postcard of the picturesque city I had loved to read about since a child. I could hardly wait to get home to describe the view to a neighbor who had been born in the area.

My fear of flying was gone. Suddenly I got up, moved past my husband, and walked down the length of the plane. I paused wherever possible to look out a window. I tried to find a place where I could stand alone in reverent silence to ask God to forgive me for having been so slow to accept the beauty of flight. Even as I realized how much I had missed in previous trips because of my fear, I knew with positive assurance that I would always be grateful for the prayer that would not go away, for it had brought me to this moment.

Take heart, friend; your prayer, too, may be answered and soon, in a way to increase your faith in God and joy in life!

A PRAYER PATTERN _____

☐ You know which is your prayer that will not go away, and whether it concerns you or some loved one, or some situation in the past, present or future. Whatever it may involve, commit it now, once again, to God and His goodness.

☐ Ask forgiveness for having failed to reach the answer sooner.

☐ Promise that you will never give up the prayer until an answer comes. There is something in this surrender that will help to bring an ultimate answer.

> *Dear Lord of the Universe, I thank Thee*
> *that I am permitted*
> *to be a part of this beautiful world.*
> *Forgive me anew for the times*
> *I have not enjoyed it to the fullest*
> *because of some fear*
> *to which I cling stubbornly*
> *and foolishly.*
> *Take from my heart the hidden fears*
> *of which I may not even be aware,*
> *so that the rest of my life*
> *may be filled with faith.*
> *Accept this thanks for the strength*
> *which comes from*
> *the prayers that will not go away.*
> *Amen.*

*"Confess your faults one to another, and pray one
for another, that ye may be healed. The effectual
fervent prayer of a righteous man availeth much."*

James 5:16

IV/We
Are Not Alone

21/Responsibility
in prayer

A n active friend who has a fine reputation for answered prayers once told me, "Never take on the responsibility of praying for someone unless you are prepared to work hard for that individual."

He said that the promise "I'll hold you in my prayers" often is made too glibly. The individual who makes the promise goes gaily on his way, never thinking of the promise again for days. Then in the evening paper he reads that the friend has returned home safely from the hospital, and he gives a sigh of relief that all went well. Or the same paper might instead publish the friend's obituary.

"I think twice before I promise to pray for someone," this busy friend told me. "I want to be sure I can be useful to him by remembering to ask for proper blessings on him and all his family."

This man is a power for prayer and a good friend to have on your side in any community venture. His comments emphasize the very practical problem of how responsible praying can be accomplished in this very busy world. When I asked for suggestions, my friend said he had learned how to enlarge his heart spiritually to include many people by using the phrase "dear ones."

Thus, when his table blessing asks God to grant health "to us and our dear ones," he is in reality including all for whom he had promised to pray. Through prayer, these people indeed become dear to his heart. For prayer enlarges the circle of those who truly matter to us.

Some people who are successful in their prayer lives feel that individuals must be prayed for by name. One of my widowed friends says, "I usually eat alone, and I keep on my tray a card with the names of those who need special help. These unseen friends seem close to me in spirit when I ask God to help them as I bless my own meal."

Another friend who also uses a written prayer list keeps it on top of a bookcase near the window. Her favorite rocker is nearby and when she sits down to rest, she picks up the list and holds it. "This is a special time of relaxing fellowship for me, for in it I discharge my responsibility in prayer," she told me with a serene smile.

You cannot pray for someone without feeling an interest in that person's welfare, which means that you think of their daily life. Sometimes this contin-ues for many years beyond the problem for which you first prayed, and a firm friendship develops.

Recently, the daughter of a friend was involved in deep trouble. She had become a member of a group of older classmates who involved her in a serious bout with the law. The experience was so unexpected that the family felt it needed spiritual help in coming to grips with it. They asked my friend if she would accept the responsibility of special prayer, as they were too involved emotionally as a family to see clearly all the aspects of the problem.

My friend agreed to take on this additional prayer responsibility as a loving gift to the family. She does not take her prayer responsibility lightly, as she reminded me, and sometimes it is hard to fit it into a busy schedule. "But," she says, "it pays spiritual dividends in loving kindness and tender friendships that can be gained in no other way." Such is the testimony of this dedicated woman whose prayers bless so many lives.

Often we hesitate to speak of prayer, and particularly to write the words "We are praying for you." Why should it be easier to send a little note into a sick room saying "Best wishes" or "Good luck" than to say "We are holding you in our loving and sustaining prayers?"

In recent years I have not hesitated to use such a prayer phrase, and the results have been interesting. A businessman telephoned me after the successful implanting of his pacemaker and said, "It was so good to know that somebody was really praying for me, and I believed you when you said you were." His words moved me deeply, and I replied that of course we had included him in daily prayer. He said, "I was in no mood for the funny cards, or the flowers, or seeing people. But I sure was in need of prayer, and I'm glad I had yours."

Many people are more hungry for prayer than most of us realize. Once we can get over the embarrassment of speaking about prayer, we may find ourselves able to give help in unexpected ways.

Sometimes in an emergency when others take the responsibility for getting an ambulance and calling the doctor, the best thing we can do is to move away from the group and engage in silent prayer.

The responsibility always is to lift the person in need to God, asking for right action at the right time in the right way. Who can know how much such a prayer will mean in helping those who are trying to find emergency telephone numbers, or waiting for help to arrive?

I practiced this technique at a social event where a friend of mine was suddenly taken ill. While she was being carried to where the paramedics waited with an ambulance, I sat in intense silent prayer for her and her husband, asking God to grant immediate guidance to those who were most intimately associated with her. Later, while she was undergoing tests, I sent a note to her hospital room to tell her of this.

She telephoned me on her first day home to thank me for my frank note about prayer. Her voice was joyous and vibrant with her love of life, and reminded me again that the responsibilities we take on in assuming loving, prayerful attitudes have overtones of joy both for the giver and the receiver.

A PRAYER PATTERN

☐ Consider well whether you wish to take on any additional prayer responsibility. Are you already taking care of all those you can accommodate in your prayer time? Is there a way you can enlarge the circle without neglecting previous promises? What leisure-time luxury can you give up to find needed prayer time? Does the answer lie in enlarging your heart so that the newcomer is indeed among your "dear ones"?

> *Dear God, give us hearts big enough*
> *to encompass all the needs*
> *that come our way.*
> *Show us how to save our spiritual strength*
> *for the true problems of the spirit*
> *by not wasting energy*
> *on trivial matters of temper*
> *and hurt feelings.*
> *Give us greatness of spirit*
> *large enough to meet the demands*
> *of our dear ones.*
> *Accept our thanks that*
> *when we assume responsibility in prayer*
> *we may turn to Thee for help*
> *in all situations.*
> *In the name of Thy loving Son,*
> *Amen.*

22/Life plateaus and prayer

Each life contains plateaus that can prove to be as monotonous as a long stretch of road across the desert or prairie, endured in stifling heat, drizzling rain or blizzard.

A family problem may seem endless, and we wonder why our life has reached this plateau. Haven't we been praying for progress toward our goals? Then why are we stuck in the sameness of routine, day after day, with no apparent movement forward?

This is a good time to recall a pertinent Bible verse that is important in building a good prayer life: "Be still, and know that I am God" (Psalm 46:10). For plateaus which slow us down and keep us from climbing mountains do offer an excellent chance to take a close look at the opportunities in current surroundings.

Plateaus have their own beckoning beauty when

recognized. I remember a morning when my husband and I were driving a friend across the desert, which to his eyes seemed "a big lot of nothing." My husband braked the car to a stop and said, "Get out and look down at your feet." I still remember the look of amazement on our friend's face when he saw that the sand was covered with tiny pink flowers so fragile he hesitated to take a step and crush their beauty.

Often we may be surprised when we discover what opportunities the dull plateau of living has to offer. And we almost always find that many of our friends are facing life's plateaus. Through such experiences, they are developing patience in facing up to long, protracted difficulties.

A young mother told me how sad she had been when she had to give up her club and church work because her son was ill. "I felt so sorry for our little boy, and I began to feel sorry for myself," she said.

Then she realized that she was coming to know her child better, to understand his likes and dislikes and to discover his talents. She appreciated her husband more because of the tender way he helped her massage the limbs of the little boy, and their family relationship improved.

Sometimes it is physical illness of our own that forces us into one of life's plateaus of seeming idleness, and we must pray anew for guidance as to how best to use this time.

One of my young friends returned from Vietnam with emotional problems complicated by physical pain. Ahead of him stretched a long period of therapy; he began in a handcraft class "to fool around with wire." One evening when we were visiting his family, he showed my husband a mobile on which he had been working. "I started to make a bird, but I guess it's turned out to be too big," he said.

My husband replied, "It's just about big enough to be the roadrunner that struts across our yard each morning, and I want to buy this for my collection of roadrunner figurines." The young man's work has steadily improved, as has his health, and he plans to enter art school soon. Persistence and prayer has paid off in restored physical and mental health, plus a new outlet for his talent.

Such benefits ordinarily do not just happen, but are the results of planning. I remember a woman in her thirties who said to me, "I knew I was going to be stuck in this dull job unless I could find some plus factor." She had gone to night school and learned a second language. Now she had a bonus on her paycheck because she could speak with members of a minority.

She did not come to this success and solution without a long period of prior discouragement. "Finally I began to pray about it. I had always wanted to travel, and it occurred to me that if I knew some other language, I could have a better time when I went to a foreign country."

Astute enough to recognize this as guidance and a way out of her plateau of discouragement, she took the first important step by signing up on registration day at a community college. It was not always easy to get to class, but she persevered, and she made her classes and learning a matter of prayer.

"I thought maybe I was not skilled enough to learn a foreign language fluently, so I asked God for confidence," she told me. Watching her speak in Spanish to a bewildered mother with small children convinced me of the wisdom of her decision, and of the good she was able to do in helping those in need.

How much did prayer have to do with her success? Without it she might not have been nudged to make the initial contact, for it takes much strength to move against the established course. A prayer for right action can lead to wonderful results, for prayer releases power and enables the individual to make a fresh start, often using unrealized resources of intellect and energy.

Plateaus are meant for the rearranging of values, and for taking a long look at what has gone before and what may lie ahead. No plateau is endless, unless we let it be so. Ahead is always the possibility of pursuing our dreams, at whatever age.

This is especially important to remember as we enter retirement. Ahead stretches a plateau without the meaning that daily occupation gives to living. It takes initiative to discover which of many projects we want to undertake to add variety to retirement living.

In any plateau period, the danger point comes when we feel that our prayers do not rise to heaven, but stay with us on a plateau of monotony. It is then that the number and fervor must be increased to overcome inertia or depression.

Keep your heart tuned to God and your eyes focused on those sharing the same plateau, making a search for daily beauty, and thus discover the way out of the endless sameness of routine. All it may take is a simple decision to explore a new trail through action, reinforced by prayer for strength and endurance.

A PRAYER PATTERN _____

☐ Admit to yourself that you are stuck on a plateau and see no visible signs of progress.

☐ Ask God to help you find a way out of the monotony of your routine. Be willing to act on the smallest sign of interest.

☐ Recognize that no plateau need become permanent in your life.

> *Dear God, please help us*
> > *to make the most of whatever are*
> > *the availing circumstances on our*
> > *present plateau of living.*
> *Keep us kind to those*
> > *who share the same situations,*
> > *and let us overlook no opportunities*
> > *for fellowship and enjoyment.*
> *Give us grace to move forward*
> > *to whatever comes next in our lives,*
> > *that we may truly know the joys of life,*
> > *and life more abundant.*
> > > *Amen.*

23/God knows your name

She sat near the back of the church and I did not know her name, but my husband and I would smile at her as we came into church, and as we left by the side aisle. Beyond a pleasant "good morning," we had never taken time to get acquainted, although we kept thinking "Next Sunday we will take time."

The "next Sunday" was delayed due to emergency surgery. It was a morning for rejoicing when my husband and I were able to return to church together to give thanks for my recovery.

This time we lingered until most of the congregation was gone before starting up the aisle. Waiting was the unknown friend.

She said to me directly, "I don't know your name and you don't know mine, but I had a feeling you had been very ill. God placed a burden on my heart to pray for you especially on the mornings I saw your husband here alone, for I could see how worried he looked."

Before I could express my thanks, my acquaintance continued, "I told myself that while I do not know your name, God knows your name, and He will know for whom I am praying."

Humbly I grasped her hand as I gave her our thanks. She knows my name now, and I know hers, and we have become good friends. In my heart I love her as "my praying friend."

Thinking about her spontaneous prayer for me has made me see how much good our prayers can do for others. We seem to forget to pray for those whose names we do not know. Perhaps this is because the circle of those whom we *do* know is also filled with those who need special prayer. Yet how will our prayers for our nation and the world be answered if we do not continue to seek solutions to widespread problems?

Many of us long for world peace, but we grow discouraged because the ravages of war are reflected in homes where fathers, sons and brothers still suffer from physical or mental wounds received in combat. While we hope for right solutions to such problems, we may become depressed and even wonder if it does any good to pray about national situations.

In all such moments of discouragement, there is great power in thinking, "God knows the names of those who need help." We do not need to know their names, but we do need to remember to take these national problems to God through the ever-present medium of prayer.

As international pressures mount, it is of paramount importance to remember that these, too, can be lifted to God. We may ask for help for nations as well as for individuals. Often the best way to pray for the large issues is to focus them through an individual need.

Always I remember a remarkable encounter in travel that enlarged my vision of how to pray about international matters. Traveling through Europe on a bus with us was a couple whose company my husband and I came to greatly enjoy as we stopped to take pictures of mountains, lakes or wildflowers. Sometimes we shared a table for luncheon out-of-doors or dinner by a fireplace.

One evening, the man seemed very withdrawn, and not like his usual self, filled with the joy of each day's adventures. It was then that he confessed that he and his wife shared a real sorrow. Their only daughter had run away from home to marry a young man who was active in a religious cult that alienated children from their parents. They longed to welcome both of them into their home, but the young people were living a nomadic life with the cult.

The couple asked for our prayers. We prayed for right action and for reconciliation, and continued to pray after we returned home, but without seeming results.

Occasionally we would receive a letter from our traveling companions, particularly at Christmas time. One letter said, "We are still waiting to hear from our daughter. All the news we have had is a terse card that we now have a grandson. How our hearts ache to see him and to hold him!" At the end of the letter, the husband had added a postscript, which is now tucked in my Bible. The man wrote: "She is my child—bone of my bone, flesh of my flesh. All I can do is to pray, wait and keep on loving her."

Reading this wistful message of human love for a dear one proved a marvelous moment in my religious life, for it showed me vividly what the Bible says in so many ways about the love of God for His human children. By his use of the Biblical phrase "bone of my bone, flesh of my flesh," the father had reminded me that we are also, as humans and children of God, spirit of His spirit.

In both the Old Testament and the New Testament we are often reminded of how God loves His children and waits for their return. Vividly I saw again God's love for all of us on our earthly pilgrimage as we make our way back to Him.

One of the avenues open to us each day on the eternal journey is the great roadway of prayer. Through it, we have instant and constant companionship, when we take our problems to the God who waits to hear our supplications.

All prayer depends upon a willingness to give of time and self in turning to God and asking for His help. As this book has tried to show, there is no one way to pray. Indeed, there may be as many different ways to pray as there are individuals. Each of us has the right and privilege to use the praying process that will help us best achieve our full spiritual potential.

As we pray, we have the inner assurance that God indeed knows our name. He waits as a loving Father to receive our petitions on our daily earthly journey toward our heavenly home.

A PRAYER PATTERN

☐ I like to think that prayer is the loom on which I am weaving the design of my life. My heart uses all the dark and bright days. The shuttle of time nudges them gently through the loom of prayer. I may be too close to the project to see the completed design, but I trust the God to whom the prayers are directed. And I believe that I shall see the finished picture in God's good time.

Dear God, please accept our thanks
for the great joy of answered prayers.
Bless and comfort the hearts of those
who continue to struggle
to overcome the sorrow of what
seem to be unanswered prayers.
Give us lasting faith to keep on praying
for the solving of personal problems
and of those in our homes, churches,
communities, the nation and the world.
With humility, we ask for that peace
which passes all understanding,
and which comes from
Thy great loving heart.
                    Amen.

You Can Make
Your Life
Count

You Can Make Your Life Count

Arthur Caliandro

Carmel, New York 1051

*This book is lovingly dedicated
to three men whose lives have
counted so much in my life:
Amos Parrish, Norman Vincent Peale,
and Homer Surbeck.*

CONTENTS

PREFACE

I came to write this book because of the excitement I feel each time I see someone expand and grow, especially after overcoming tremendous odds such as recovering from a failure, learning from a serious mistake or taking on a great responsibility.

The ideas set forth in this book really do work. They are taken directly from the lives of a number of people who've tried and tested them and, in the process, have found the key to a more victorious life. I commend these experiences to you in the sincere hope that they will help you to turn on your growing power and to keep on growing as others have—that they will help you to *make your life count!*

FOREWORD

This book tells how to grow and develop as a creative and effective person and it describes the growth process in a fascinating and persuasive manner. The flow and variety of the text will keep your interest sustained until, regretfully but appreciatively, you come to the final page.

Dr. Arthur Caliandro is eminently qualified to write about personal growth. To his native gift of insight into human nature has been added a comprehensive professional training that has made him one of the most competent students of personality in the Christian ministry today. He knows people and understands how to inspire them with the touch that makes personality respond. His is the rare gift of bringing out of others the great potential inherent within them.

Since I've been privileged to observe Dr. Caliandro's techniques over the years, I've found him to be a motivator of people—one who effectively stimulates in others a real desire for growth and helps them learn how to get started in the growing process.

Yet, with all his accomplishments, Dr. Caliandro is a man of sincere humility who also is in a never-ending state of growth—a quality which has endeared him to all who know him. His book is filled with moving incidents and real-life stories of individuals who've found the way to a richer and more rewarding life, illustrating the profound victory that can and does emerge out of weakness and defeat. Truly evident in this book is the remarkable power that changes people from what they are to what they were meant to be.

Dr. Caliandro, a gifted and eloquent preacher in the tradition of practical Christianity and its life-changing qualities, is also a loving and caring friend to many, whether encountered in person or through the pages of this inspired book. The measure of my confidence in this man may be inidicated by the fact that when I sought a colleague minister at Marble Collegiate Church and someone to ultimately carry on its work, I was fortunate enough to be led to Dr. Arthur Caliandro.

Norman Vincent Peale

PART 1

How to Give Life Direction

Brethren, I count not myself to have apprehended: but this one thing I do, forgetting those things which are behind and reaching forth unto those things which are before, I press toward the mark for the prize of the high calling of God in Christ Jesus.

Philippians 3: 13, 14

INTRODUCTION

I didn't start growing until I was thirty-three years old. As I look back, I wasn't aware of my lack of growth then. I wasn't aware of many things. I didn't dare mention this insight to anyone for a long time, and finally when I did tell a close friend, he responded by saying that he knew what I was talking about because he didn't start growing until he was thirty-five years old. I was astonished and gratified not to be alone with what I thought was a singular malady.

Since then I have mentioned this thought to many other people, many of whom readily identified with my experience. People would frequently admit to me that they'd been thirty or older before starting to be aware of life and of themselves in their relationship to it.

It all began for me on a January Sunday in 1967 when I first approached the pulpit of the Marble Collegiate Church in New York City to participate in a worship service. It

3

seems that through all the years before that day, I had been in an incubator getting ready to grow up. Not that I hadn't been active and moving ahead personally and professionally. I had been. But things had not come together within.

When I'd accepted the invitation of Dr. Norman Vincent Peale, pastor of the Marble Collegiate Church and the church's board of elders and deacons to become a member of the church staff. I'd done so with a mixture of excitement and apprehension. I'd been flattered to be invited to the great and historic church located on Fifth Avenue in the center of the nation's largest city. On the other hand, I wondered what I was getting into.

This was such a long way from the tiny mission church in Portland, Maine where I was born and reared, the second son of a Methodist minister. Ten pews of the huge New York sanctuary would more than hold a full congregation of the little church situated on the first floor of an old frame house just a few blocks from Portland's waterfront. Also, it was in sharp contrast to the church I had just left in Brooklyn where most members lived close enough to walk to church and the entire staff consisted of the minister, a sexton and a part-time secretary.

I had arrived at a church where thousands worshiped each Sunday, coming from all over the world, and where the church staff alone, if seated in my father's Portland church, would almost fill it! There were so many people from various backgrounds. And there were many more activities and programs.

I was there less than a week when I realized I was in over my head. I had not known before how much I *didn't* know. Responsibilities were assigned to me—handling correspondence, relating to groups, helping people—where I had no experience and little idea of how to proceed. I stood in a pulpit with a three-and-one-half-century tradition of excellence and power. Its most notable preacher, Dr. Norman Vincent Peale, was still preaching regularly to thousands of expectant listeners. Hence, I quickly became aware of my limitations as a preacher as well.

My greatest desire was to measure up, but I truly didn't know if it would be possible. Three months into my tenure I was so uncomfortable that I developed headaches, nausea and even chest pain. I was sure these symptoms were emotionally engineered but to be certain I had a complete physical examination. The doctor confirmed the emotional genesis of the symptoms. It would have been easier, I thought, if he had found something physically wrong.

During this rocky personal time I didn't dare tell anyone what was going on inside of me, not even my wife, Gloria, to whom I can say anything and who has an uncanny sense for getting to the heart of a problem. I did a lot of serious praying, however, and I scanned the horizons of my heart to discern what God might be saying. After a while I began to sense a message. "Arthur, you've wanted to be a minister ever since you were a little boy. You always looked up to your minister father. You are doing what you're supposed to do. You have a lot of energy and you want to do well. You have always wanted your life to count for something. But you're never going to be what that inner drive says you ought to be unless you start growing. You have much to learn. This place is great for growing. Get going. Face what you should be facing. Learn what you have to learn. Or leave."

I stayed.

Soon after coming out of the crisis with the physical symptoms, I was invited to be the administrative minister and to direct the church staff and its program. I was pleased with the confidence shown in me, but again I'd had no experience with administration. I was especially nervous at staff meetings where my insecurity was compounded by the fact that I was the youngest person there.

5

Since I had decided to stay at Marble, I adopted a private slogan which I often repeated to spur myself on when I faced a challenging situation. It came from my desire to improve. I would tell myself, "But a man can learn and grow, can't he?" This phrase kept me going time after time.

Three years into my Marble experience, Dr. Peale said, "Art, I have been preaching two services for many years. Now I think I had better do just one sermon each Sunday. Will you take the first service?"

"Thank you for the confidence," I said, "but no, thanks."

Again I was encouraged and flattered, but frightened. This was the opportunity of a lifetime for a young minister. Although I dreamed of being a preacher who could communicate the gospel message with clarity and power, I had to admit I was only mediocre. It would be unfair to the congregation and unwise personally for me to share the pulpit with one of the most effective communicators of the century. Dr. Peale seemed to accept my refusal and dropped the subject.

Then, a few months later, he brought up the subject again. "Art, about preaching the first service," he began. "My doctors tell me that I need to pace myself if I want to keep on preaching. Since I want to continue, I am going to be sensible about it. I want you to take the first service." This time it was a command.

It is a great opportunity, I thought. *On faith I should try it. Maybe this is what God wants for me and for the church. But I'm afraid*.

My fears were endorsed the day it was announced that the preaching responsibility would be shared, when an outspoken member of the congregation said to me, "I hear you're going to preach during the first service."

"Yes," I said, "do you have any thoughts about it?"

"You won't last long," she replied, "You'll be sacrificed."

"Ouch!" I thought. "She may be right." Yet as quickly

as the thought came, I remembered my phrase, "But a man can learn and grow, can't he?"

Although the congregation was supportive during those early months of my preaching, I was not confident that I was doing well at all. I was making a real effort, but trying hard often isn't enough. A close friend came to me one day and, with words carefully selected and designed to avoid hurting me, suggested that I develop skills other than preaching. His suggestion crushed me, and for the first time I found myself saying aloud what I had said so many times silently to myself: "But a man can learn and grow, can't he?"

Soon after that conversation I purposely obtained some help with my public speaking and started the long road toward growing up as a preacher. And now when I look back on the years as a minister at the Marble Church, I see the pains of those early months and years as labor pains, necessary preliminaries to the birth of a man who was seeking to grow.

Someone once told me he saw the Marble Church as a laboratory for living. Another said the church is like a garden because of the beautiful way in which people grow there. I gratefully endorse both descriptions, because it is the place where I started my growth both as an adult and as a Christian, where I started to make my life count!

I am learning every day from my fellow travelers. It seems as though every time someone tells me about the power of faith in his life, my faith is strengthened and increased. When someone speaks about the healing of a broken relationship, I am inspired and encouraged. When a person shares an insight into himself and embraces life more lovingly, I, too, am stretched by his growth. That's what this book is about—people and their problems and how they overcame them and grew—how they, too, made their lives count.

CHAPTER 1

Go-Getters Get Goals

I WAS ON MY WAY out of the church one Sunday afternoon when a certain lady grabbed me by the arm and said, "Arthur, I know you're in a rush but I need a word." We ducked into the side corner of the sanctuary where we could talk. I looked at Cindy, a highly intelligent and able saleswoman for a sportswear company and thought, *she's the kind of person I would like to have in my company if I were a sales manager*. Still I could tell something was very wrong.

"I almost called you this week," she said. "I'm so depressed."

"Why didn't you call?" I asked.

"I have to learn to handle my problems, especially this one," she replied, frowning.

"What do you have to handle?" I asked. "What's the problem?"

"My job—it really has me down," she went on. "I'm

9

not going anywhere. I want to do well, but I'm not sure what I should be doing. I've prayed, talked to people, read, but I can't seem to find the answer."

Quickly I evaluated the situation. Cindy is a committed and serious Christian who prays. And she's a good person, kind and sympathetic. She's generous, sometimes almost to a fault. What could be wrong?

"Do you know what you want, *really* want?" I asked her after a few moments' pause.

"No," she answered. "I know I want to do well and to make a difference somewhere. But I don't know what I really want."

"Then you don't have any goals. Is that right?"

"I guess not," she said. "I just want to get out of the mess I'm in."

"Well, that's a good start," I told her. "But you're going to have to be a little more clear than you are now about what you want."

I remembered what a psychiatrist friend once told me about his work as a therapist. With almost every patient he spends some time answering what he calls the basic question of life—what do you really want? He prods his patients until they find the answer. Then, he finds, they are on their way toward solving many problems.

"Cindy," I said, "this is the beginning of February. Do this. Focus your thoughts on December 31, the last day of the year. Believe that by then you will know what you want and that you will have a new job. Fix that idea solidly in your mind. Pray, talk to people and learn as much as possible about yourself and what you can do. Know that by the end of the year you will find what you want and need."

"Are you sure this will work?" she asked.

"I'm sure," I said. "It has worked for me and I've seen it work for many others.

"Okay, Art," she said. "I'll try."

What Cindy was experiencing that day is an age-old problem, that of finding one's destiny—God's plan for one's life. Each of us struggles with it until the problem is solved—until we find the solution which is right for us, which is consistent with our talents and our interests. Then the power to grow is unleashed and we're on our way.

This happened to Dr. Peale who, as a preacher, lecturer and author, is one of the most energetic men I have ever known. His schedule would tire any man half his age. I've known him to speak in New York in Sunday, California on Monday, Arizona on Tuesday, Chicago on Thursday and Columbus, Ohio on Friday. And he packs the house full at every meeting. He zips through his schedule like a runner in a fifty-yard dash. What's his secret? Beside healthful living, he has found a goal—the right goal for him. And he's had that goal since the day when more than forty years ago, he spoke to a group of New York businessmen at a luncheon in the University Club in New York City.

The luncheon was held in the main dining room of the club, an impressive place with mellow oak paneling and a high, ornate ceiling. On that day, the room was filled with young businessmen in their twenties and thirties, a good-looking group with all the sophistication of the Ivy League. Many of those men were destined to become business leaders in New York and in the nation.

As they talked during lunch, Dr. Peale made an enlightening discovery. He asked the young man on his left where he went to church.

"I don't go to church," he said. "I sometimes attend on Christmas and Easter, though. But my wife goes regularly."

Dr. Peale addressed the same question to the man at his right and got a similar response. "I go once in a while," the man said, "and I see to it that my children go to Sunday school by driving them every week."

Few, if any, of the men at his table had any interest in

religion and few of them ever went to church. They might not have been turned off but they certainly weren't turned on by spiritual topics.

Dr. Peale began to wonder about the other men in the room. What were they like? He surveyed their faces and sensed a cloud of spiritual apathy enveloping them. He asked the man next to him, "Are they churchgoers?"

"Some are," the man said, "but I don't really think you could call this a churchgoing group."

"What in the world are these men going to do when they are confronted with the problems of life and have no spiritual resources to draw on?" he asked himself. "What's going to happen to our country if these men don't have the Christian experience and the Christian ethic to help them when they face the temptations that fill every business day?"

Those questions bothered him. He knew there was a great human potential in that room. It needed only to be developed. And it could be developed in one of two directions—the right way or the wrong way.

Clear as the sun against a cloudless blue sky, Dr. Peale saw his goal. He would bring the gospel of Jesus Christ to businessmen everywhere in a way they could understand and appreciate. He would share with them a practical Christianity which would help them with their everyday problems. Most of all he would introduce them to the truths of the Christian faith. He would make everything he said so exciting and appealing that they could not forget it.

Dr. Peale did just that. He started by speaking to as many groups as he could. Some were large, many small. And he excited people. The result: He did what he set out to do and thereby became one of the most effective spokesmen for God anywhere to businessmen all over the world.

It would have been easy for a preacher such as Dr. Peale to look at that group of businessmen and say to himself, "These men certainly have a problem. I don't think I've ever seen a group more apathetic about religion. I had better skip the religious talk as it will probably only bore them. It doesn't seem that one man can do much to change them. Maybe I should forget this group and find a more congenial one."

Many able, but timid, people have been frightened away by big problems and challenges. Yet, the most successful people I know are those who recognized a human need that was not being met, evaluated the problem and decided to do something about it. They discovered their right goals and expanded and stretched as they grew toward the challenges of those goals.

There is a right goal for you, one especially made for you. It is yours alone, uniquely yours, and you alone can discover what it is. Others may help by making suggestions or pointing you in the right direction, but ultimately you alone must decide what is right for you. The knowledge must come from deep within yourself and it must be right for you.

How will you know when it is right? You will know when it meets these two tests. One is the test of time, when over a period of weeks or months it continues to feel right. Secondly, it must be helpful and good for other people.

In a way, discovering your right goal can be likened to the experience a man refers to when he says he has been called by God to become a minister. *Your* right calling is just as much from God as is the minister's. It is the call of your destiny, bringing into focus what you are supposed to be and to do with your life.

So often the call to the right goal emerges when a person has a problem which needs solving and then sets out to solve it. The result is growth, often *phenomenal* growth, because problems are not just problems—they are growth motivators!

CHAPTER 2

Eyes Ahead

A FRIEND WITH CONSIDERABLE EXPERIENCE in the publishing field looked at the outline of this book, noticed the first section was to be about goals and asked, "You're going to write about goals?"

"Yes," I said, "why do you ask?"

"Don't you think enough has already been said about goals in other books?"

"Probably," I agreed.

"Maybe you ought to reconsider including such material," he suggested.

I thought about that for a minute, and then replied, "What anyone else or I may say about goals isn't new. It has all been said. But I find every time I preach a sermon on goals I get more positive responses from the people than with almost any other subject. More surprising was the response I got when I recently spoke to a particular sales organization about goals. Many of the people were steeped in goal-setting, yet person after person said after the talk, 'I needed to hear that again. I get lazy and my goals tend to get hazy. The subject of goals may not be new, but it's sometimes helpful to be reminded of them."

"All right," he said, "Go ahead and write about goals. But start your chapter with what you just told me."

Recently a brilliant physics student, a young man on his way to a great career, told me of the very first time he ever went to church. He was fourteen years old and his mother had brought him to hear Dr. Peale at the Marble Collegiate Church.

"Dr. Peale wasn't there that Sunday, and you preached," he said. There was a pause. I didn't know what was coming next, an expression of disappointment or a kind word. "You told a story which I still remember," he continued. "In fact, it has helped me immeasurably in getting through school and in facing all the troubles I've ever had."

I perked up immediately. Amazing, I thought. That would have been eight years ago, for he was twenty-two at the time.

"What was the story?"

"It was the story of three boys racing in the snow," he replied, smiling.

"You're kidding" I said. "I remember that story and how I almost didn't use it. It seemed too simple and elementary."

"Thank God you used it," he went on, "because it helped put me on the right track."

Here's the story as I told it that Sunday morning.

Three boys were playing in a snowy field. The snow was deep and they were having a great time rolling in it. A neighbor paused to watch them, then called out, "Hey kids, would you like to have a race? I'll give a prize to the winner."

A race seemed like a good idea to the boys so they gathered around the man to get their instructions. "The winner," he said, "will not be the one who runs fastest, but the one who runs the straightest line. I'll go to the other side of the field and give a signal, and then you race to me."

He went to the other side of the field and shouted, "On your mark, ready, set, go!" The boys took off. The first one looked at his feet as he ran to make sure they were pointing straight ahead. The second, worrying about how straight the boys on either side of him were running, tried to line himself up with them. But the third youngster understood the game. He kept his eyes fixed on the man at the other end of the field. He had his eye on the goal. He didn't waver from a straight course, and he won the race.

The two losers in the race had fallen victim to two common problems which cause us to be distracted from our goals. The first is self-consciousness, excessive worry about one's self with too much concentration on mistakes and weaknesses. The second is a person's worry about what other people may think, concern about what and how he's doing.

A few days after the physics student told about the effect of the story upon his life, I decided to use it in a speech which I was to give at a real estate sales meeting. After the speech, a woman who had just received an award for selling more than $1,000,000 worth of real estate came up to me. "Thanks for telling the story about the boys in the snow," she said. "It's exactly what I needed to hear."

There's another story with the same message which appeared in *Christian Science Monitor* several years ago. It tells about the amazing effects of keeping your eyes on the goal.

Ted St. Martin, a dairy farmer from Washington State, achieved a distinction in basketball which no one is likely to exceed for a long time, if ever. Although he's not a member of a basketball team and doesn't even play regularly, Ted is the most accurate basketball shooter in the world.

One afternoon Ted St. Martin sank two hundred successive baskets from various parts of the basketball court. On another day he set out to see how many successive foul shots he could make. The most consecutive shots made by a professional player was fifty-six—made by Bill Sharman, formerly of the Boston Celtics. Standing at the foul line fifteen feet from the basket, Ted St. Martin sank nine hundred twenty-seven straight shots.

Incredible! How did he do it? Here is his explanation. Don't concentrate on the ball. Keep your eye on a spot on the back rim of the basket. In other words, keep your eye on the goal.

After reading the story I was so intrigued by the idea that I had to try it myself. I went out to the driveway where there is a backboard and basket, focused on a spot on the back rim of the basket and surprised myself by sinking several shots. My heart began to race with excitement. My younger son, Chuck, watching my performance, decided to test the idea, too.

"You're not supposed to concentrate on the ball," I said as I handed it to him. "Forget the ball and concentrate on a spot on the back rim of the basket."

He aimed the ball. *Swish.* It dropped into the basket. Now he was excited, too. "Let's see if we can do five in a row," he said.

A few minutes later he had made five, then six, seven, eight, and nine. The excitement was too much. He ran into the house to get his mother so she could watch. Then he came back and made twenty-two straight baskets! It took me a little longer, but I finally matched his twenty-two.

Then, silently, I made a father's wish. If Chuck can exand his talents so successfully in this basketball exercise, I hope he learns as he grows older that he can grow in many other ways by simply keeping his eye on the goal.

It's good to be reminded again and again that the best way to reach a goal is to keep an unwavering focus on it. And it's a great way to stimulate growth as well.

CHAPTER 3

Good Goals Are Movable Goals

KNOWING I WAS WRITING a chapter on goals, a friend sent me an article from U.S. News and World Report with the following note attached. It makes so much sense I am including it here. "Arthur," he wrote, "consider this. Goals sometimes change. A goal for one stage of life may not be right for the next. As we grow we change, and that sometimes means finding new goals."

This friend writes with authority I respect for he is firmly established in a second career. In his first career, which took him through his forties, he was a teacher. At present he is an executive in an advertising company. It seems that I am meeting more people who are involved in mid-career changes, often involving considerable risk and sacrifice. Yet, the satisfaction and growth realized by the changes are usually more than equal to the investment.

There should be some comfort in the last words of my friend's note. "Life is always moving," he wrote, "and that's all right as long as we do what Oliver Wendell Holmes suggested when he wrote, 'One thing I've found out about this life is this. It's not so much where we stand but in what direction we're moving.' "

The U.S. News and World Report article is a fascinating account of two men who, because of their growth, changed their goals and started going in the directions they determined were right for them. One had been a vice-president of General Motors. His income had exceeded five hundred thousand dollars a year and he'd had a chance to become president of the company, one of the world's largest corporations. Yet he quit and took a job as president of the National Alliance of Businessmen, an organization which helps small businessmen, especially minority groups.

His reason for making the change, he said, was that the corporate position would have kept him from doing what he really wanted to do with his life.

The second executive had been the head of a stockbrockerage firm in Atlanta until several years before the stock market began to have trouble. At that time he decided to quit his brokerage job and later become a maintenance supervisor for the city parks in Atlanta. His explanation for changing careers was that he'd had a craving to get back to nature. He tackled the new job with a brand new goal—to make the parks under his supervision the most beautiful ones in America.

Both of these men were successful in highly competitive fields. Yet they both realized that they had achieved what they wanted in their careers, and that the goals which had challenged them for so many years were not valid for the years ahead. They needed new goals to keep growing.

Change isn't always easy. It involves breaks with familiar ways and places. It may mean going into unchartered waters. But God never promised that life would be easy. If anything, God is urging us on to bigger and better things. He delights in nudging us out of lives too comfortable and too complacent into new and challenging situations. He urges us to change our goals when we find we're miserable with the ones we have, and He does it so that we can grow and keep growing. And it makes sense when we realize that the alternatives to growth are decay and deterioration.

My wife, Gloria, and I once were invited to a luncheon given by an older woman for a group of her college friends. Since they'd graduated a half century earlier, we were expecting to have to listen to several hours of reminiscing about what happened 'way back when they were starting out in life.

We couldn't have been more wrong. During the luncheon, the hostess asked each of us to tell what we were currently doing with our lives. Alma, the woman next to me, was a gracious person in her mid-seventies, with sparkling eyes and a soft but lively voice. She began to tell about herself. After she was widowed and had retired, she'd planned to move to Florida where she had bought a house. Just a few weeks before she was to move, however, she received a call from a friend who worked with the blind in Philadelphia.

"Will you come and help us out?" asked the friend.

"Oh, I can't do that," Alma protested. "I'm moving to Florida—permanently."

A couple of days later, the same friend called back. "Please give us just a little of your time."

"All right. But I'm moving to Florida, so I can't help for long," Alma repeated.

Taking a few hours from her day, Alma began to help. She soon discovered she could make an important difference in the lives of several people, and this made her very happy. "I wonder if God is telling me something," she thought. The months passed and Alma kept putting off her move to Florida, feeling she just couldn't leave.

"I'd come to realize," Alma said, "that I was in just the right place for me. There was so much to be done and I had the skills to do the job. I felt so good inside I just couldn't leave when they needed me so much!"

As I heard Alma tell her story, I couldn't help but think how young she sounded. She had thought she was ready to retire, but God's plan for her life showed her that she had more growing to do. She discovered that years don't matter when you have a goal for tomorrow—and when the goal is right for you.

The person with the right goal is like a sailboat in a strong wind. A friend of mine, formerly in the Coast Guard, described what he'd seen the tall ship, *Eagle,* do when under sail in a storm. He'd been on a Coast Guard cutter accompanying the *Eagle* across the Atlantic at the time.

"We were following a little behind the *Eagle,* under restraint of partial power so we wouldn't leave her," my friend said. "The day had been exceptionally clear and calm, a few gentle swells and breezes—not enough to make much progress. But on the horizon I could see black clouds. A storm was heading our way. In a matter of minutes the storm hit, sending waves crashing over the deck and spraying everybody and everything with cold salt water. Despite the sound of the storm, I could hear the booming snaps as the *Eagle's* sails filled with wind and bulged forward with fury. It was energy, raw energy, wild energy and the *Eagle* trapped it all.

"Before we knew what was happening, the *Eagle* took off across the ocean. She seemed to leap from one huge wave to the next and the harder the wind blew, the faster she went. She was in her element. That magnificent ship was made for the big wind—and in our cutter we couldn't begin to keep up with her."

Isn't that the way it is when you find your right goal? It's like having the wind at your back, filling you with energy—raw energy, strong energy. And regardless of how rough the seas around you might be, you know you're moving toward that goal. A person goes best and grows most when he finds his right goal!

CHAPTER 4

Priorities, Please!

ONE AFTERNOON FLORENCE PERT, Director of Lay Activities at the Marble Church and also my close friend, came into my office, closed the door, sat down across from me, and in her thick Alabama drawl said, "Arthur." I knew by the tone of her voice that she was about to suggest a correction in my way of doing things. I braced myself and listened.

"It seems to me you attended a lot of meetings here at the church last week," she said. "Like every night." My first reaction was to defend myself by telling her she, of all people, should know how important meetings are. Then I had second thoughts. "That's right," I said with a slight air of aloof martyrdom, "why do you ask?"

"Was that the best use of your time?" she asked. "Did you really need to be at every one of those meetings?"

"I guess not, Florence," I said. "But you know how it is."

"I sure do know how it is," she said, "but do you think

23

that's what God wants you to do? For your own good, for the good of the church and for your family's sake, don't you think maybe you should reconsider your priorities?"

She was right on target. I needed to hear those words—"what God wants . . . reconsider your priorities." I had fallen into the same trap again that had prompted a similar conversation many years before with a grand-motherly lady named Mrs. White, when I was a college student.

Mrs. White had watched me for some time one sum-mer while I was working as a camp counselor and had seen how completely caught up I was in the spirit of cooperation with the campers and the staff. In fact, I was so cooperative it seemed I couldn't say no to anybody. No matter what the request or how it interfered with my plans, I always said yes.

One day when I had just finished saying yes to a request which could have meant postponing my job as-signment, Mrs. White called to me. "Young man," she said, "come here a minute. I want to talk to you. Do you want to talk with me?"

Now that seemed like an odd question, but she knew me well enough to know what my answer would be. "Of course," I said obediently.

"When I finish," she said, "you may not be so agree-able. In fact, you may not even like me at all."

"Oh, my goodness," I thought, "what's coming next!"

"When I was your age," she began, "I was just like you. I couldn't say no to anybody. You're a good guy, always trying to please everybody, but you're not nearly as effec-tive as you could be. Do you know what the word 'priority' means?"

I was embarrassed, but I nodded that I did.

"Okay," she challenged me, "what does it mean?"

She's a tough one, I thought as I began to fumble for

words. I couldn't find any that made sense. Finally I confessed, "I guess I really don't know."

"You sure don't," she said. "But I'm going to tell you. 'Priority' means choosing the thing that is most important for you to do and then organizing your life so that you do it."

With that explanation, Mrs. White began to help me line up the priorities for my summer job. It would have been easy for me to get angry with this interfering woman. But what she said I could not deny.

When we finished and I was about to leave she smiled and said, "Now remember, when you have your priorities lined up the right way, saying yes or no will be almost automatic." I nodded and started to walk away.

"By the way," she called out to me, "aren't you planning to be a minister?"

"Yes ma'am," I said.

"Well, if you don't believe what I said about priorities, I want you to get a Bible and see what God has to say. The Bible is really big on priorities."

Now I was afraid she was going to ask me questions about the Bible. I was so embarrassed I couldn't remember much beyond my name, and I certainly couldn't recall Bible passages.

"Yes, I want you to read the Bible," she said. "Turn to the Ten Commandments where God tells Moses what comes first. Look at the first commandment where God says *He* comes first. (Exodus 20:1-6) And then read what Jesus had to say about priorities. 'But seek first His kingdom and His righteousness, and all these things shall be yours as well.' (Matthew 6:33) Always remember those priorities!"

"Wow!" I thought as I finally got away from her," she really turns it on when she wants to make a point."

However, both Florence Pert and Mrs. White were absolutely right when they spoke of the importance of

25

priorities. We can be intelligent, important, well-liked, good-looking, and decent—everything going for us—but if we don't have a set of right priorities which we live by every day, we're never going to reach our goals. We'll fall far short of our dreams.

There's another lesson about priorities, one just as important as knowing what your priorities are. I learned this one from the owner of a camera store.

A couple of years ago when I was in a camera store in Portland, Maine, I met a man who had obviously grown to the point where he could work through problems by sticking to his priorities. It was a Saturday afternoon. There were only two workers—Bert, the store owner, and a girl who served as clerk and cashier, in a rather large store. Since I needed the advice of the owner I leaned against the end of the counter to await my turn. I found myself listening to Bert's exchange with his customers. He was friendly and patient and gave them his total attention, even when some of their questions were patently naive and even ridiculous. Then the telephone rang, and the girl called out to her boss, "It's for you."

Barely interrupting the conversation with his customer, Bert asked the girl to take the number and say he would call back. When my turn came, I complimented him on the way he'd handled the telephone call. He thanked me and then began to talk with me as he had with the other customers.

"Until a couple of years ago," he said, "my life seemed to be dominated by the ring of the telephone. I would run to it on demand. Sometimes at the end of a day, it would seem that all I had gained was a case of frazzled nerves from dashing back and forth to the phone.

"Finally, I decided to establish some priorities, because things weren't working out well. I decided that the most important people to my business were those who came into the store and wanted my attention. So now, I give them my first attention. Still I also know how important the telephone is to my business. I frequently have to say that I'll call back, and I always do.

"But ever since I decided to give my first attention to my customers in the store and have refused to let the telephone run my life I've been happier, my life is more orderly, and my business has improved."

Let me ask you some questions. Who's setting *your* priorities? Other people, events, the situation around you? Are you making your own decisions about what you should do first or are you setting your priorities by default? Are you letting anybody or anything which seems to need your attention get in the way when you should be doing something else? Do you ever consider what God might want for you?

When I think about questions like these, I realize my priorities must be a conscious choice—my choice based upon what God wants for me. I'll never be what I am meant to be or reach my goals until I take charge of my priorities. And you'll not reach your goals until you do the same for yourself. When you decide what's most important in your life and put it first, you'll be like the owner of the camera store—happier, better organized and more successful.

CHAPTER 5

Take Charge!

SEVERAL YEARS AGO I needed to make an administrative decision which I knew was right and had to be made. I prayed about it and felt I knew what God would have me do. But then I hesitated and rationalized, avoiding responsibility because I was afraid I might displease someone. Actually I was hoping the problem would solve itself or perhaps someone else would solve it for me. While I procrastinated, however, I helped make the situation worse.

A wise friend, Amos Parrish, known to friends as A.P., invited me to lunch one day and challenged me with a concept which intrigued me then and has helped me ever since.

"Arthur," he said as we drank our coffee, "do you know the game of baseball?"

I thought that was a strange question since A.P. knew I was an avid baseball fan. But I know A.P. seldom raises such questions unless he intends to make a point. So I went along.

"Of course, I do," I said.

"Then tell me what the pitcher does," he challenged.

"Why, he throws the ball to the batter."

"Right. Now tell me what the catcher does."

"He stands behind the batter and catches the balls the batter either misses or chooses not to hit," I said.

"Right again," A.P. said. "You know, baseball is a lot like life. Some people are the pitchers. They take charge of things. They throw the ball. They're in command and the success of the game of life depends most on them. And then there are the catchers, people who don't make the decisions. They are on the receiving end, catching whatever is thrown at them."

I was beginning to understand A.P.'s lesson. He knew exactly what my problem was. I had to take charge. I had to learn to be a pitcher.

"There are times in life when we have to pitch," he said, "and there are times when we have to catch. But when you want to do someting with your life, you've got to take command and be the pitcher. My suggestion to you, Art, is that you learn to pitch, because if you catch all the time, everything will be thrown at you and you're not going to like or be able to handle a lot of it."

I've thought about and acted upon A.P.'s suggestions many times. And he is absolutely right. What he was really telling me was, when a goal is right, go after it. Pitch! Take charge instead of accepting indecision and timidity. If you have authority, use it right, but *use* it. Don't worry so much about whether you please other people or not. That's the most common reason for timidity and indecision. People tend to respect the person who takes charge and makes decisions. Instead, set high standards and move toward them. Grow toward your standards!

One of the best examples I ever witnessed of a person taking charge was a man who had almost no formal education. Several years ago, my wife, Gloria, arranged a real adventure (a term to be translated, "be sure to do all the things which most of the other tourists don't do") for our family as part of a South American trip.

Our adventure began at dawn when we started out in a rented car, driving down the left side of a bauxite road into the jungles of Surinam, a small country on the northeast coast of South America. After about three hours on that red dirt road, we had passed nothing except scattered native huts and vast tracts of tropical rain forest.

Finally we reached the spot where the road ended on the bank of the Coppename River. From there on the trip would be by dugout canoe, the only non-native feature of which was a 35-horsepower outboard motor. Even the natives had to give way to progress, and Gloria wasn't about to persuade them to paddle when they didn't have to.

We traveled for three hours along a wide jungle river where the banks were lined by dense vegetation broken only at the point where there was a tiny native village. Except for an occasional flock of macaws high in the tops of the towering trees, the jungles's stillness was disturbed only by the sound of the outboard motor for most of the trip.

Once we passed a tree whose branches jutted out into the river, and on the end of one branch there was a strange-looking bird with an enormous beak.

"Look!" I cried, "I wonder what kind of bird that is!"

"It's a toucan," my sons said in unison.

My mouth gaped in startled surprise. "How do you know what kind of bird it is?" I asked, not really convinced they did.

"It's on the back of every Froot Loops box," the boys explained with exaggerated patience.

At last we reached our destination, a small cabin built in the Amerindian style with woven walls open near the top so the breeze could blow through. We unloaded our gear and turned to find a man about four feet ten standing outside the door. His name was Marius, and in broken English mixed with *taki-taki,* the native language, he told us he was our guide and we were immediately going to take a trip across the river to see an interesting sight, Raleigh Falls. It would be only a three-mile hike, he said, and it would help prepare us for the ten-mile hike through the jungle scheduled for the next day.

We climbed into the motorized dugout canoe and headed out into midstream, traveling toward the rapids that lay upriver. Suddenly we heard a frightening sound. The motor sputtered, then went dead, leaving us with no power to navigate the rapids. As we swiftly drifted toward a group of large rocks Marius grabbed a paddle and, with what seemed like the strength of ten men his size, maneuvered the canoe to a rock. Then he pulled the bow up on the rock and secured the canoe. I offered to help, but Marius declined, correctly estimating about how much help I would be.

With a combination of wild gesturing and broken English, Marius indicated he needed a hairpin. Gloria, as it turned out, had brought everything she could think of other than a hairpin. Undaunted, Marius unsheathed his machete, used it to pry a nail out of the canoe near where the motor was secured, cut the nail in half and pounded it against the rock until it was shaped like a cotter pin. Then he inserted it into a tiny hole in the propeller shaft of the outboard motor. He started the motor and we were on our way again.

When we reached the other side of the river we started off afoot through the jungle. Marius's idea of walking was more like our jogging. We marvelled at how easily Marius, barefoot, darted among the trees, machete poised in one hand. By the time we reached the falls, the sun was sinking behind the treetops. Marius indicated we would have to hurry for it was dangerous to walk through the jungle in the dark.

We started back, but before we could reach our canoe the sun had set and dark shadows lined the jungle floor, dim even in the middle of the day. Suddenly Marius stopped and turned around, then began to push us back down the path.

"Snake," he said tersely.

I looked, but could see nothing except the shadows across our path. With two swipes of his machete, Marius deftly felled a thin palm tree about ten feet high and cut off its branches. By now we could see the snake, large and brown, coiled up in the middle of the path.

Marius struck the snake with the palm tree until he was sure it was dead. Then he tossed the serpent to one side. "Bad poison," he muttered laconically.

That night as we sat in our cabin recalling the events of the day we were suddenly struck, for the first time, by the danger we'd faced. We realized at the same time that we had been on one of the safest walks in our lives despite the danger, for we'd been with a man who was truly in charge of himself.

Marius never forgot he was the pitcher, even for a moment. He knew exactly where he was going and what he had to do to get there. And he knew what was required of him in the face of danger—the protection of his hikers.

Marius was equal to his responsibility. He was a reliable guide. We'd sensed his maturity, his capability, even when sitting in the midst of the rapids with no power for the canoe. Marius was in control, and we were confident and secure. And because Marius was a "take-charge" person, we're alive to tell about it!

CHAPTER 6

Have Patience – And Persistence!

SOME CELEBRATIONS ARE SPECIAL and this one was no exception. There were no decorations, fireworks or crowds of people. It was only a quiet lunch in an ordinary restaurant in New York City, and there were just the two of us—Gene, tall and angular with graying hair, smartly dressed in blue blazer and red-and-blue-striped tie, and myself. Despite the simplicity, it was an event I shall always remember because of what I saw and heard that day.

After we found a table and placed our orders, Gene began to speak, in characteristic short, clipped sentences.

"Arthur, you've known me for a long time," he said. "During most of that time, my life has been a struggle. Before I met you, I'd made and lost a fortune. And when I came to New York, I had to start all over again." He glanced down momentarily, then faced me again.

"Do you remember the first time we had lunch

together?" he asked. "I do because of how uncomfortable I felt. I didn't have enough money to pay for the meal. And as you talked, I kept wondering whether you'd pick up the check. You can't imagine how relieved I was when you did!

"That wasn't the only time I was broke. Many times during the past three years I've lived from hand to mouth, not knowing where my next meal would come from. But things are different now. My business is doing very well, and so am I. So let's celebrate!"

Things certainly were different now for Gene, I agreed. This cheerful, relaxed man didn't look anything like the fidgety, preoccupied person who'd sat across the table that day three years ago and told me about his plans. In relatively short time, Gene had completely rebuilt his life.

"How did you manage to come so far in only three years?" I asked.

Gene's answer was simple and straightforward. "I found out that if you know what you want, and what you want is right for you, you need only go after it. Stick with it even when the going is rough, and in time it will come. That's the principle I applied. But I don't think I could have made it without regular worship and prayer. The spirit of my church helped keep me motivated. I guess you can say that I made it by the power of God."

What Gene was describing—the attitude that had worked so well for him—was nothing more than faith and persistence—his strategy for getting back on his feet. The same formula that Gene used will get results for anyone else who earnestly tries it. Determine what you want. Make sure it is right for you. Be sure it is spiritually sound; ask God's blessing on it. Then, patiently and persistently, pursue your goal!

Persistence and patience pay off in productivity and in personal growth. Each new challenge brings another opportunity for both.

34

I saw a most vivid example of success through patient persistence by a most unlikely character in a most unlikely place—a campground in the Grand Teton National Park in Wyoming where Gloria and I and our two sons, Paul and Chuck, were camping one summer.

Our camp was located in one of the most beautiful spots I have ever seen, a little place called Leigh Lake. The lake was no more than two and a half miles long and a mile across at its widest point. Trees were everywhere, and the view looked as it must have looked ten thousand years ago —fully developed by God and virtually untouched by man.

Across the lake rose snow-covered peaks—Mount St. John, Mount Moran and above them all the Grand Teton, its majestic pinnacle reaching 13,776 feet into the sky, a hundred feet higher than Switzerland's famed Jungfrau. The sky was clear blue, and you did not have to look up to see it. Sky and mountains were reflected in the cold, still water of the lake.

At that early hour of the morning, the only other creatures I took notice of were the birds, a tiny chipmunk looking for crumbs near the ashes of last night's fire, a few other reluctant campers a good distance down the lakeshore and a solitary little black ant.

He walked in front of my foot, his legs moving in a quick, easy rhythm. I had really never watched an ant before, but I recalled that the Bible mentions the ant several times. Ants are supposed to be wise, resourceful and socially very highly organized.

I thought it would be interesting to test this insect's wisdom and resourcefulness. First I made a little hill in the sand. It must have seemed like a mountain to the ant. He walked along without breaking stride and went right up the hill and down the other side. Then I dug a little hole to make a valley across his path. He went down the valley and, again without stopping, marched up the other side. Next I took a stone and put it in front of him. He tried to climb the stone, struggled a bit, fell back, reconsidered the situation, then walked around it.

This little ant was passing some tough tests. I decided to try one more obstacle. I put a twig in front of him. He struggled with the twig until he also found a way over it.

During all those trials, what did that little ant do? He kept moving. At no time did he stop and consider himself to be in bad circumstances. He did not complain. I did not see him go to another ant and tell him how bad things were. Nor did he go to the government of the ant colony and ask it to solve his problem. That little ant knew what his task was. He saw every obstacle only as another challenge, and he continued to walk through his obstacle until he arrived at his goal.

This little creature gave me an impressive lesson in persistence and patience. He knew how to do only one thing—to keep on going. He was never overwhelmed by the obstacles. And he didn't give in to feelings of fatigue. He seemed to realize it would take time and effort to get to his destination, and he kept going, patiently and persistently. To me his patient persistence made the difference between an ordinary ant and the extraordinary creature he was.

People who patiently persist, undaunted by obstacles, usually get ahead—and *grow* as they go. Their lives *count!*

PART 2

How to Make the Most of Each Day

This is the day which the Lord hath made. We will rejoice and be glad in it.

Psalms 118:24

INTRODUCTION

How does one make the best use of one of life's greatest gifts, the gift of today? Today is all we have. Tomorrow hasn't happened yet and yesterday is gone. We have only a memory of yesterday and a dream for tomorrow, but we don't have either one. All we have is today. And one of the great challenges of living is getting each day into the proper perspective so we can make good use of it.

You would think that after a few years' experience people would become more expert at using their days. But many haven't. It appears that people always have had a problem getting hold of the *now.* Jesus referred to this problem when He taught his listeners not to be concerned about tomorrow because there was enough to deal with today. (Matthew 6:34) And when He said to a prospective disciple, "Let the dead bury the dead," (Matthew 8:22) He meant to leave the past behind where it belongs. The psalmist referred to living today when he wrote, "this is the day which the Lord hath made." (Psalm 118:24) Note he didn't say *yesterday was the day or tomorrow* will be the day the Lord hath made. This is the day.

I must confess that I spent a good part of my life living in the future. I would work and plan for the day when things would be better. What would be better? Everything would be better. My church would be stronger and greater. I would be more effective in everything I was doing. I would have time to spend with my wife and children. I would travel and read and do all kinds of things. That was all going to happen some day. In the meantime I had to do what had to be done. One day would run into another, undistinguished.

One evening not long after I had gone to Marble Collegiate Church and had finished a day packed with all kinds of activities, I came home late. My wife, Gloria, understandably upset that I was late again, met me at the door with the comment, "Well, I see you're finally home." Before I could take my coat off she began, "Arthur!" I knew I was in trouble. She calls me Arthur only when she's angry; otherwise it's Art.

"Do you know what you have done today?" she asked.

"Of course I do," I said. "I've been very busy at the church." Then I continued with some of the details of the day's activities.

"Now *I'll* tell *you* what you did today and what you do every day" she said. "You go around chasing your own shadow. You eat too fast and never enjoy your food. You're always on the run. You may be building a church, but you seldom appreciate what's happening at any given moment. That's no way to live. You're missing life."

"You don't understand," I defended, although I knew in my heart she was right.

"I understand only too well," she corrected me.

After a few more minutes of this exchange, I softened a bit and said, "All right. Assuming you're right, what do you think I ought to do?"

"You might start by paying attention to each moment and seeing the value in what you have right now," she said quietly.

That confrontation started me on a fascinating but somewhat difficult growth struggle involving learning to live each day. I started to observe others and to learn from them. I found that growth takes time. It requires effort, struggle. There are often steps backward after achievement. It's a push-pull process which, if kept in motion, will result in great change. But I learned the most from an illness which left me with the profound realization that there might not be a tomorrow, that today is all I might have.

Doctors discovered that I had a serious blockage in one of the arteries of my heart. It would be necessary to do a coronary artery bypass. I didn't accept this news easily for I had always congratulated myself on being healthy. I had never been sick except for an occasional cold. I'd always had tremendous energy. And besides, I was too young, only forty-five years old. The news stopped me cold.

Then I learned another lesson. It often takes something dramatic or even catastrophic to make us stop and think. I can still hear the words of the doctor, "Thank God you had a warning. A siren went off in your system. You were lucky."

And my reply, "But what caused this problem?"

"Several things," he explained. "One of them is probably the intense life style you described to me. These conditions take years to develop."

"I've changed my lifestyle," I assured him lamely.

"But maybe you need to make more adjustments," he went on.

As it turned out he was right and I'm still making them.

There were many lessons to be learned from that ordeal, one of the most important being a profound appreciation for the moment. Now. Today.

Although I'm planning to see many more tomorrows, I'm not letting today slip by as I once did. I have been to the brink where there was almost no tomorrow and I've learned that today is all we really have and we must make it count.

CHAPTER 7

One Day at a Time

A FEW DAYS BEFORE I was discharged from the hospital following my operation my surgeon, Dr. Eugene Wallsh, who is head of cardiovascular surgery at New York's Lenox Hill Hospital stopped in for his daily visit. I'd come to love and respect this talented and dedicated doctor not only for his skill as a surgeon but also for his sensitivity as a human being. He takes the time with his patients to tell them what to expect, what they are likely to feel and how long pain will last. Such advance counsel is extremely helpful and comforting. During our visit he issued a warning. "When you get home you'll probably get depressed."

"How's that?" I responded with surprise.

He went on, "Most people do become depressed after this operation. Your system has had a major shock and there are many adjustments you must make. Healing takes a long time. People often get depressed in the process. Just expect it, and one day it will pass."

43

I thought of others I had known who'd had the same operation, and recalled they had gone through some depression. Although I am not depressed often or for long, I assumed this would be a big one and that I'd just as well accept it. After getting home I waited for feelings of depression to come. One week, two weeks, a month. At last I started back to the office part time. The depression never arrived.

Finally, I mentioned the overdue depression to my wife, wondering aloud what had ever happened to it.

"Do you realize what you did?" she said. "You never gave it a chance to get started. You got up and got dressed from the first day you came home, even though you napped a great deal. After breakfast you wrote your feelings about the hospital experience in that note book, remember? That in itself was therapeutic because you expressed many deep feelings. You spent an hour each day reading the Bible and copying down verses. Then you worked on your book. You had a realistic plan for each day, and you followed your plan. The depression never had a chance."

It was then that I reminded Gloria, not too humbly, of the big change that had taken place since that fateful day early in our marriage when she'd confronted me with the fact that I was chasing my shadow.

The idea is to live *one day at a time*. I'm convinced that if I can grasp the idea and practice it, anybody can. Unfortunately that simple, common-sense concept isn't so simple when we are faced with an enormous and overwhelming task. To avoid being overwhelmed, what is needed is the clear, simple discipline of doing only what we can in a day — every day — knowing that if we take only one day at a time, we can accomplish wonders.

One of my good friends, a likeable and talented man who is always doing something for others, seems to be continuously frustrated with himself. He says he always has too much to do. He never gets anything done on time and rarely finishes what he starts out to do. In our frequent conversations, he is usually talking about what he didn't do yesterday or what he is going to do tomorrow. But he rarely gives concentrated attention to what he is supposed to do today. He's a living example of the old saying, "When you've got one eye on yesterday and the other eye on tomorrow, you're sure to be cockeyed today." As a result, he is always frustrated.

Sometimes when I get caught up in anxiety about the enormity of a task ahead of me and become frazzled, someone in my family is likely to remind me about the story of the clock in an old McGuffey's Reader. I am usually regulated by remembering it.

Once there was a clock which sat on a mantlepiece for many years, ticking away the time. As the clock approached the end of the year, it started to think about how many times it would have to tick in the coming year. It figured it would have to tick exactly 31,536,000 times. The figure was simply overwhelming, and at last the clock said, "I can't do it," and stopped. Then someone reminded the clock that although the number of ticks was staggering and seemed impossible to attain, it had only to do the job one tick at a time. Well, that made sense to the old clock, and so it started up again, ticking away the minutes and the hours —one tick at a time.

The moral: Take life one "tick" at a time.

The great Canadian physician and thinker of a generation ago, Sir William Osler, had a similar idea for handling anxiety-producing situations. Osler suggested that people learn to live in "daytight" compartments, which are analogous to watertight compartments. In a watertight compartment, the capacity is limited. You fill it to capacity, cap it securely and know that the contents will stay inside.

In a daytight compartment, the capacity is also limited.

45

We put into one day only as much as one day can hold, recognize the limit and then decide we will not allow the contents of that day to spill over into the next. While we are in our daytight compartment, we focus all of our energies on the business at hand. We do not ignore either the past or the future, for today's business may be related to each, but we realize that the present is all we have to work with. We live in the present, and grow in the present.

Dr. Osler suggested a technique for making the daytight compartments really daytight. Draw a circle, he said, around a twenty-four-hour period. Determine what you can do in that time, then don't bother your mind with anything outside of that.

When the pressures become great, as they will sometimes do, a twenty-four-hour period may be too long to comprehend. If so, circle just one hour and live within it. If the hour is too long, circle a five-minute segment.

Regardless of how large or how small the segment of time you choose, finish what you plan for it. And then move on to the next compartment. Before you know it, you will have completed the task at hand. And you will have discovered you can get much more accomplished than you ever dreamed.

Dr. Osler's idea has had a profound effect on me. Often when I find myself overwhelmed by demands and tension rises in me I will think of daytight compartments. I will circle an hour or, if necessary, a five-minute segment, visualizing what I can do well in that much precious time. And then I do it. I find this idea truly works.

I don't worry about the five minutes after that, or the next hour, or any of the minutes or hours that have passed. There is nothing I can do about them. But there is something I can so about the moment at hand, the wonderful *now*. I can make each moment count—and so can you.

A friend, while touring Italy, visited a cathedral which

had been completed on the outside only. When this man entered the cathedral he found an artist kneeling before an enormous wall upon which he had just begun to create a mosaic. On some tables nearby there were thousands of pieces of colored ceramic. Speaking in the language of the Italian artist, the visitor asked how he would ever finish such a large project.

The artist answered that he knew what he could do in one day. Each morning he marked off an area to be completed that day, and he didn't worry about what remained outside that space. He would take one day at a time, the best he could do. And one day the mosaic would be finished.

In one respect, we are all like the Italian artist. There is only so much we can do well in one day. But the days accumulate until finally we can achieve our objective.

To grow we need only make each day count, one day at a time.

CHAPTER 8

Shortcut or Shortchange?

AN IMPORTANT COMMENTARY on progress in the years since the beginning of the industrial revolution is the story of the successful shortcut.

The driving force in industry has always been speed and efficiency—doing things faster, easier and at a lower cost. The quest for speed replaced the horse with the tractor, the buggy with the automobile and the stagecoach with the diesel. Such shortcuts serve to benefit humanity.

Shortcuts in basic human processes such as personal growth, however, are quite another matter. Taking a shortcut only because of impatience and the desire to move ahead more rapidly can prove destructive. Any attempt to shortcut growth can result in serious trouble.

We often become impatient when we want something. We prefer to rush to our goals rather than move at a slower pace, taking one step at a time but achieving greater personal growth. Part of the problem is that our minds are so much quicker than our ability to perform. We can think of all kinds of things we would like to be or to do. Thinking takes only seconds, but becoming what we think takes time—a long time in some cases.

For example, a skier standing at the top of a slope ready to make his first run may see in his mind an Olympic star flying gracefully and confidently down the slope. "That is what I want to do," he may say to himself. He may even try. He may start out confidently, make one or two turns as he picks up speed coming down the slope, then suddenly—*crunch*. He falls flat.

The skill of an Olympic star takes years of hard work to acquire because there are no shortcuts to excellence. Such skill doesn't come with the first try, perhaps not even with the first thousand tries. Like the Olympic skier, you must work and grow before you can solve your problem easily and achieve your goal. And that takes time, patience and persistence.

The late Evelyn Underhill, an Englishwoman writing about spiritual growth, realized this truth. "We wish for things to happen fast," she said, "but real growth, the kind of growth which comes from the inside out, is far more gradual."

Surely when Jesus was frustrated by the slow and apparent lack of growth in His disciples He wished He could do something to force men along. But He knew they would be right only when they themselves grew from the inside out, step by step.

A few months ago I talked with a fifty-year-old man from Los Angeles who was on a business trip to New York. He had come to the Marble Collegiate Church to discuss a personal problem.

"Until three years ago," he told me, "I was the financial vice-president of a large corporation. I earned a good living and everything in my life seemed to be going just fine. My wife and I were happy. And my two daughters, with whom I've always had a great relationship, were doing well in college. I was active in my church, holding an office and sometimes teaching in the Sunday school.

"About four years ago, some men I had known for a long time came to me with a business scheme which they were convinced would make all of us millionaires in a few years. They seemed intelligent and capable and they had been successful in business, so I listened to them. They wanted me to invest in an enterprise which, although new, seemed to have a great potential. After talking with them at some length I was convinced we could succeed together. So I left my job, invested my money and went into business with them.

"It took about six months before I realized that something was definitely wrong with the business," he continued. "These men were doing things which were on the verge of fraud. When I questioned them about their practices, I always got the same reply: 'We're only doing this until we get over the hump, and then we'll straighten out.'

"They never did straighten out. Fortunately I had enough sense to keep out of direct participation in their dealings. Soon, however, they became involved in something else—playing around and cheating on their wives. I got caught up in that myself.

"Nothing seemed to go right, and before we knew it the business collapsed. The government started an investigation and not long after, my wife asked me to move out.

"Ever since my business and my personal life collapsed, I've spent hours agonizing over the problems I created for myself," he said. "There were so many mistakes. But the biggest one of all was my belief that I could get rich by taking shortcuts. Our idea seemed so good at the beginning, but the shortcuts finally caught up with us. Of course, I never really fooled anyone but myself with all of those big ideas."

I asked this man what he was doing to rebuild his life. "At first," he said, "I thought of suicide. I had embarrassed so many people and made such a mess of my life. But the more I thought about suicide, the more I thought of my wife and my daughters. I knew I couldn't do it. I wanted to make things up to them.

"I went home and asked my wife if she would take me back. She agreed. Then I went to my minister and told him what I had done. He prayed with me and arranged for me to see a counselor. Now I have another job and am starting all over. I haven't quite put the pieces together again, but I'm working on it. I've always heard that a person could get practical help with problems at this church," he told me, "and I need all the help I can get."

In the midst of all his problems, this man had gained one profound insight into life—shortcuts can be destructive. He and I reviewed again the fundamentals of persistence and patience. In nature everything has its time and place. One step is a building block for the next. And each step must be allowed to proceed to its maturity before the next one begins. Slowly this man made his trip back to sound living.

There is harmony to life if we allow ourselves to grow naturally. Henry David Thoreau, the naturalist and essayist, said, "Nature never makes haste. Her systems revolve at an even pace. The buds swell imperceptibly without hurry or confusion as though the short spring days are an eternity."

Nature never makes haste because nature knows,

even if man does not always believe her, that there is a right rhythm and pace which produces the best results. Any other process is likely to invite problems.

Not long ago I heard the mother of a teenage girl say of her daughter, "If only she could skip these teenage years and become a mature adult tomorrow without all this struggle!" Having teenagers of my own, I could appreciate what she was saying. There are times when I wish the same for our sons, but in reality I know that taking such a shortcut would cheat them. They will grow best if they experience every stage of life, slow and painful though it may be.

Struggling to solve problems without easy answers does something beneficial for a person. Struggle can't help but build strength and endurance. It refines a person, enabling him to take the stresses of life and use them as catalysts for growth. Such growth eventually builds that precious commodity called wisdom.

Alfred Russell Wallace, a scientist who developed a theory of evolution at the same time as did his contemporary, Charles Darwin, once observed an emperor butterfly trying to get out of its cocoon and wrote this about it. "It struggled, pushed and pulled for a long time until finally its body emerged fully. The butterfly rested momentarily, fluttered its wings and then flew away." Wallace then wondered what would happend if he helped the process, so he cut open another cocoon and waited for the butterfly to fly away. Instead, the butterfly crept moodily about, drooped imperceptibly and died.

The struggle to get out of the cocoon, Wallace discovered, was nature's way of helping the butterfly to develop. The struggle required exactly the pace and sequence of growth necessary for the butterfly. Without this struggle the butterfly never acquired the delicate strength it needed to survive.

Often the shortcut seems a welcome relief. But is it really? Can we afford to be deprived of the strengthening and growing process that shortcuts eliminate from our experience? This is the question we must ask ourselves.

CHAPTER 9

A Job Well Done Is Done Right!

WHOM DO YOU REMEMBER when you think of those who had the most lasting influence on your life? Most people, when asked, will mention a parent, a teacher, a minister, or a special friend. When asked why they remember a particular person, they will usually say it is because the individual helped them to set high standards for their lives, either by example or by expectation, or both.

When I asked myself those same two questions, the people who came to my mind first were my father and an English teacher. In addition to a lot of love and care, my father gave my two brothers and me a set of high moral standards. I can remember so vividly hearing him say as one of us would leave the house to go somewhere with friends, "Always remember who you are." He meant, "Always live up to the Christian standards you've been taught, wherever you are."

I remember my English teacher, Miss Ruth Sturgis, at

Portland High School in Maine. Miss Sturgis was so exciting. At first I didn't like her because of the demands she made on us. I thought she was mean. She made us work hard. Her purpose seemed to be to do things right in her class or not to do them at all. It was obvious from the first day of the year that we were going to do many assignments for her and that we were going to write and rewrite until at last we met her expectations. But I also remember how pleased I always was when I made a good grade, because then I knew I had achieved a high standard.

We appreciate and remember most those who have helped bring out the best in ourselves and who helped us to set high standards for the quality of our lives.

Of course, the best model for a high quality life is Jesus Christ. Everything He did and taught related to living the best possible life. We need go no further than the Sermon on the Mount to discover what we must do to live what He considered a good life. In it, He speaks of relationships—with God and with other people—and of high personal standards. He reminds us of how important standards are: "You have heard that it was said, You shall love your neighbor and hate your enemy. But I say to you love your enemies and pray for those who persecute you. . . ." (Matthew 5:43-44) We are shaped by the levels we choose to reach.

John Gardner, a former head of the U.S. Department of Health, Education and Welfare, tells of asking an extraordinary music teacher about his success in producing outstanding students. "I teach that it is more rewarding to do a job well than badly," the teacher said. "Many have never been taught the pleasure of setting standards and then living up to them."

There is no substitute for doing a job right, whether it is playing a musical instrument, creating something beautiful, doing a particular job, or relating successfully to another person. And there is never a good reason to settle for less than the best. But we have to first determine to excel, then actually perform whatever work is necessary to result in the best that we're capable of.

I recently had to have the trim on my house repainted and asked painters to submit bids. John, the painter who got the job, was a middle-aged man who not only appeared honest and whose references checked out, but who also stated that he would personally supervise the painting because he liked to have his jobs done right.

John lived up to his word. He saw that every window and every shutter was painted meticulously, and his relationship with his employees indicated that he took great pride in his work and in his reputation. When he finished, I was so pleased that I asked him about another bit of maintenance that needed to be done on the house. John said he couldn't do it but he referred me to someone who could. I called the man and when he'd finished I saw that he did the same kind of good work that John had done. He smiled in appreciation, then said, "There are some painters I never like to get referrals from. They do such sloppy work. But not John. I always like to follow him, because I know he does things right and people are going to be happy with him. I've never heard a complaint about any of his jobs. That makes it easier for me."

The quality of the work each of those men did impressed me but there was something else about them I particularly noticed. They were calm, pleasant men who obviously enjoyed their work and they were pleased with themselves because they knew they were doing things right. They had grown up to excellence. Beyond the personal growth encouraged by the high standards they set for themselves, their businesses were growing as well. They realize that people want the best and they've learned to produce high-quality results.

One of the most successful corporation lawyers of our time, L. Homer Surbeck, told me about the first job he ever had. As a boy in his native South Dakota, he'd worked for Chris Andersen, a truck farmer who specialized in growing onions and cabbages. Homer would work ten hours a day, hoeing vegetables for ten cents an hour. Sometimes, when the summer temperatures were in the nineties, Homer would feel a great temptation to skip a few chops with the hoe or to kneel a little longer and rest before moving on down the row.

"One day a wonderful thing happened," Homer said. "I looked up, and far off in the distance stood my boss, Chris Andersen. I imagined that he was standing right by me, looking at me. After that, every time I was tempted to do less than the best, which is what he hired me to do, I imagined my boss there at my elbow."

After the harvest was in Chris Andersen visited Homer's parents. He told them what an excellent crop he had had that year and credited Homer with much of his success. "You know," he said, "that boy of yours works just as hard when I'm not there as when I am."

Homer brightened when he heard that. "Mr. Andersen," he said under his breath, "if only you knew. I could feel you at my elbow all the time."

After telling that story Homer went a step further. He said that one of the most important discoveries of his life came when he realized that Jesus Christ lived in him. He said that it is comforting and inspiring to know that the Holy Spirit is always with him. As a boy he imagined Chris Andersen at his side and it helped him do a good job. And now, as a man, he is elevated to a life of excellence by the power that comes only from the presence of Christ, from the Holy Spirit within. Can there be any better source of inspiration and strength for personal growth and accomplishment?

CHAPTER 10

Honesty – The Best Policy

JUST AS THERE IS NO SUBSTITUTE for excellence, neither is there any substitute for honesty. Dishonesty blocks growth, defeats the desire to make a constructive contribution to life.

Several years ago I received a phone call from a man who began the conversation with these words, "Dr. Caliandro, how would you like a fine-hundred-dollar donation to the church?"

Few ministers would want to turn down such an offer. I felt like saying, "You need to ask me a question like that!" But something in his voice made me hesitate. Also, I knew he had never contributed to the church before. Instead of instantly accepting, I asked hesitantly, "Sam, what's the occasion?"

"Well, maybe I shouldn't ask you," he offered, "but . . . ." His voice trailed off uncertainly.

"But what?"

"Do you suppose," he ventured, "that you could give me a receipt dated two years ago?"

"You mean you're being audited by the IRS and you claimed a five-hundred-dollar donation to the church without giving the money?" I speculated. "Is that right?"

"You got it, Doc," he replied.

"As much as I would like to help you, you know I can't do that," I told him. "But why don't you come in to see me, and let's talk about it."

The next day Sam, trim and neatly dressed and in his late twenties, came to my office. His usually relaxed manner was replaced by one of worry and tension as we talked about his problem with the Internal Revenue Service. I had known Sam for years, and I knew what would happen to him if I followed his suggestion. The extra tax he was going to have to pay would not hurt him nearly as much as his guilt in avoiding his rightful responsibility.

I advised Sam to tell the auditor the truth, to say that he had made an error in judgement and now wanted to set things right. "If you approach the auditor as I suggest, you will feel a lot better about yourself," I told Sam. "And I predict the auditor will help you work out your problem."

A few days later Sam phoned me again. "Doc, I just finished my audit, and you won't believe what happened. I told the truth, and you were right. I felt better immediately, even while I was preparing myself for the penalty. The auditor was great. He said he wished everyone would come clean. Then he worked with my tax return, finding things I could have claimed but didn't. I ended up paying just a little more than I had originally figured.

Sam learned the spiritual truth Jesus taught when He said, "Blessed are those who hunger and thirst for righteousness, for they shall be satisfied." (Matthew: 5:6)

A dear friend, retired from a successful career in advertising, said to me one day as we walked down Fifth Avenue in New York City, "If I have learned anything in life, it is that when you walk toward the light, your shadow is always behind you. It's never in your path." Sam had never heard these words, but he'd certainly learned the truth of this statement. Sam had made the decision to do what was right. He didn't compromise. Although it was difficult and the temptation was great to do otherwise, he lived up to the best within him. He grew in stature. His self-esteem was strengthened. No guilty conscience will ever haunt him. It is often difficult to do things right, but doing them right pays dividends.

I've always liked and have been helped greatly by this story. A rich man once noticed the miserable living conditions of a certain carpenter and called the man to him. "I want you to build a house for me," said the rich man, "but before the job is yours, I want you to draw up a set of plans and give me an estimate of the cost."

The carpenter did as the man requested. Everything looked good on paper, and so the man said, "The job is yours. You may begin work immediately. I won't be here while you are building. I have to go away on a business trip and won't be back for several months. I will expect the house to be finished when I return."

The carpenter was glad to get the job because he needed the money. As soon as the rich man left town, though, he promptly put aside the plans he had shown his employer. He began to cut corners, to skimp on materials, to hire inferior workmen for lower wages than those budgeted and to cover his shoddy workmanship with plaster and paint.

When the house was finished the owner had returned, the carpenter went to him and presented the keys. "I've done as you asked," he said. "I've finished building your house."

The rich man took the keys, then unexpectedly returned them to the carpenter. "They are yours," he said. "I had you build the house for yourself and your family. This is my gift to you." The carpenter regretfully realized that it was only himself whom he had cheated.

Just a simple story, but it tells us something very important: We must not settle for less than the best in what we do. The quality of life can be no greater than that of our own standards and actions. In one sense, we *are* no greater and no less than our standards. Anything less than complete honesty lowers our aspirations and diminishes us as persons. Honest people have a greater growth potential. They make a valuable contribution to the world.

CHAPTER 11

Worry Wastelands

ONE OF MY GOALS is to reach such a level of trust in God and in myself that I will never again worry about anything. I still have a ways to go, but I've also come a long way. I credit the progress to all I've learned since hearing Dr. Peale say many years ago that it isn't *necessary* to worry and that with God we can overcome whatever causes worry.

Worry has never solved a problem. It has never helped any situation, anywhere, any time. Worry does nothing but compound our problems. And when we look closely at the meaning of the word *worry* we see why. The word comes from the old English word *wyrgan* which means to strangle. And that is just what worry does. It strangles us, cuts off our creative energy.

Although worry is not the least bit helpful but rather is wasteful and destructive, people keep on worrying and keep on suffering. Since the beginning of time people have been worrying, even though it causes them to have all manner of aches and pains as well as the more serious problems of heart disease and ulcers.

Dr. Charles Mayo of the famed Mayo Clinic said that he had never known anyone to die from overwork but he'd known many people who literally died from worry. The poet, Robert Frost, wittily explained why. "The reason why more people die from worry that from work is that more people worry than work!"

If worrying is not helpful, why do we do it? There are many reasons, but this one is probably most applicable: We worry because we are not aware that we don't have to worry. We don't realize there is an alternative. One which provides a way to successful living— one which has been tried and proved by thousands of people. Here's how you can apply that alternative to your own life.

First, develop a constructive philosophy of worry, a set of beliefs which will put worry in its proper perspective and give you some right insight for handling it. One such belief has already been suggested—facing the fact that worry never solved a problem. Another is to recognize that worry is a common problem and to handle it, we need to get it out in the open where we can successfully deal with it.

Comedian Jerry Lewis said he once talked to his doctor about some of his problems and when he finished the doctor suggested, "Jerry, don't worry."

"Doc," Jerry replied, "how do you *don't worry?*"

Jerry had a point. Sweeping worry under the rug does not help at all. Worry does not go away; it only stays out of sight. It remains a nagging nuisance. And just telling a person not to worry does not usually help either. The doctor's comment left Jerry Lewis in a quandary. The advice was intended to comfort, but what could Jerry do with it?

A much better piece of advice is this. Admit something is worrying you, get it out in the open, then decide to do something constructive instead of worrying.

Leslie Weatherhead, the late English preacher and author, said that worrying is like putting an engine in neutral, starting it, then pressing hard on the accelerator. The worrier expends a tremendous amount of energy, but he goes nowhere.

Jesus talked about the same thing. "Which of you," He said, "by being anxious can add one cubit to his stature?" Worry will not do you any good. It is a fruitless and debilitating activity, and you need to recognize it for what it is.

Eric Butterworth, well-known author and teacher, has made yet another observation about worry. Dr. Butterworth defines worry as just another burden. If you have a real problem, it alone is burden enough without weighing yourself down with still another. If you were already ill, Dr. Butterworth says, would you take something which would further upset you—eat out the lining of your stomach, give you a headache or make you tense and irritable? Of course not. Yet, that is what we do when we have a problem and then we treat it with worry. We simply add another burden.

We dare not take on that burden. Instead we must adopt a constructive philosophy which recognizes that worry cannot help but can only aggravate the existing problem. Then the second step in the alternative to worry is to start to clarify the problem by getting the facts.

A number of years ago I was chaplain at the Hermann Hospital in Houston. One day I received a frantic call from a nurse. "Will you please come up and see Dave right away?" she insisted. "He is worried he's going to die."

As I entered Dave's room I understood clearly why the old English word for worry means *to strangle*. Dave's face was ashen, as though no blood were going to his head. His lips were taut. As I approached his bed, his glazed, fearful eyes stared beyond me into space.

"Hi, Dave," I said. "What's happening?"

"I'm going to die," he said flatly.

I had visited Dave several times and knew him to be a highly emotional person who had a tendency to be despondent. "Let's start at the beginning. Tell me what's happening," I said.

"I'm going to die," he repeated, this time choking with emotion. "I have cancer and I'm going to die."

"Dave, did the doctor come by to see you?" I asked him.

"Yes," he nodded miserably.

"And what did he say to you?"

"He said I have a tumor."

"What else did the doctor say?" I asked quietly.

Dave winced. "He said there is a possibility it's malignant."

"You say 'possibly malignant,' but is the doctor sure?" I asked.

"He's not sure, but he thinks it might be."

"Did the doctor say anything about treating the tumor? Can he operate?"

"Yes. He says he can operate and can probably get all of it out."

We continued to talk until Dave finally moved beyond his emotional reaction to the bad news and was able to sort out the facts. Then his problem began to take on a new perspective. Certainly his condition was one which would cause him, or anyone else, great concern. But concern is quite different from worry. Dave finally acknowledged that the facts were serious, but that he could and would deal with them. His new attitude of concern was much more constructive than his former one of worry which had produced such a hopeless, fearful outlook.

As I left to go, Dave said, "Thanks. I'm still concerned, but that's a lot better than worrying. I'll pray about this. Will you pray for me?"

We prayed that Dave's surgery would be successful

and that he would be healed. As things worked out, Dave regained his health. And he learned from his experience the valuable lesson that clarifying a problem and being concerned are much better and much more effective than simply worrying about it.

The third and final step in developing an alternative to worry is this. Substitute prayer for worry. During the last week of Jesus' life, He faced problems as difficult and as painful as any man will ever face. Yet there is no evidence that he ever worried about them. On the night of his betrayal, according to the scripture, he went to the Garden of Gesthsemane to pray. There He followed the sound advice He knew from the scriptures and from His Heavenly Father, to "Cast your burden on the Lord, and He will sustain you . . . ." (Psalm 55:22)

Jesus prayed a prayer of release in which He turned his burden and Himself over to His Father, " . . .not as I will, but as thou wilt." (Matthew 26:39) That act of release of His will and the acceptance of the power of the Holy Spirit working through Him gave Jesus the ultimate courage—the courage to face the Cross.

To sincerely pray and release your own will and preference is often difficult. But it is also a rewarding prayer, because when you turn yourself completely over to God, you thereby remove the obstacles which impede His power to work through you. You cannot pray that prayer of release while worrying. Worry indicates that you still want to try your own solutions and control your situation. Worry, however, is a negative force which cannot exist where God's power operates. Faith and worry are utterly incompatible.

In a simple, everyday situation I once learned about the power of prayer as a substitute for worry. I was working on a sermon on worry when I took a break to look for some important papers which had to be mailed that day. I turned my office upside down and searched through just about every conceivable place in my home, but I could not find the papers.

I knew I had seen the papers in only two places, my office and the office of the man who had given them to me. Perhaps they were there. I called him. His secretary said he was out but was expected back at any minute. She said she would have him call me.

An hour passed. I became more and more agitated. This man was usually prompt and reliable in returning calls. Why hadn't he called me? A second, then a third hour passed. The post office was about to close, and I had to get those papers!

Then I remembered hearing him talk about buying some airline tickets. So that was what had happened! He had gone on a trip and was probably in such a hurry he had not had time to call. His secretary must have been confused or else she was just trying to be reassuring.

Worry began to work on me. I got a sharp headache and became depressed, and even started to panic. Maybe I should call him again, I thought. But that will only irritate him when he finds it out because he prides himself on his promptness in answering his calls. That will make him think I don't trust him. All kinds of conflicting thoughts were going through my head.

When my worry reached a peak, I suddenly felt as though someone had given me a hard jolt. "What in the world are you doing?" I asked myself. "Here you are, preparing a sermon on worry, and you're doing all the things you're going to tell other people not to do!"

That realization calmed me down a bit, and I began to think about the points which I'd planned to develop in the sermon. Point one deals with substituting prayer for worry. I decided to put my recommendation to work.

I sat down in a chair and began to pray. "Dear Lord, please help me with this problem. . . ." My mind began to clear, and my body started to relax. I felt better. Now it was time to put feet on my prayers. God will reveal the solution to the problem but He expects us to do our part.

The next thing I did was pick up the telephone and call the man who'd never returned my call. It was a risk, but I decided that solving my problem was worth it. When he answered the telephone, his first words were, "Am I glad you called back. I've been trying all afternoon to get you but your phone was busy."

I had had a series of phone calls, and he must have called at the same time as the others. The first part of my worry had been groundless. It was based on feeling and not on fact. Then I explained that I could not find the papers he had given me, and that they needed to be mailed that same afternoon.

"No problem," he said casually, "I have other copies and I'll drop them in the mailbox on my way out of the office."

The problem was solved in a matter of two minutes when at last I decided not to worry but to pray for God's guidance and then to do something constructive.

When we take a good look at worry, we recognize that it is pointless and fruitless and only creates an additional burden at a time when we are least equipped to handle another problem. Who needs it?

CHAPTER 12

Quit Quitting

ONE OF THE WORST THINGS that can happen to any one of us when we face a big problem or a tough day is to become a quick quitter. Sometimes, as soon as a major problem appears, we tend to give in to pessimism and run from the problem. All of the hopeless, angry, negative thoughts we can muster come to the fore and seem to take control of us. We are defeated before we begin to put up a fight.

Did this ever happen to you? If so, you know from experience that you're defeated because you gave up hoping. Without hope, we cannot solve problems satisfactorily. Without hope, dreams cannot come true. Hope is one of the master keys to growth, because it keeps possibilities alive.

Some of the best teachers on the subject of hope are athletes. Hope reigns supreme for good athletes for without it victories just don't happen. One evening I turned on the television to watch the final half of a basketball game between the New York Knickerbockers and the Milwaukee Bucks. Milwaukee then had the top-rated team in the nation, led by the talented seven-foot-two-inch giant, Kareem Abdul Jabbar. With the speed and agility of a deer, Jabbar was sinking basket after basket, and his team was winning.

With five minutes left to play, Milwaukee led by seventeen points. Under normal circumstances they would have coasted to victory. But that night Milwaukee was up against something else. The New York players were not quick quitters. They would not give up hope for victory until the final buzzer had sounded, ending the game. And so they proved that nearly anything can happen in five minutes *if you believe it can*. While Walt Frazier and Earl Monroe dazzled the capacity crowd at Madison Square Garden with magical ball handling, stealing the ball from the Bucks and dribbling through their defense to score points almost every time they threw to the basket, Dave DeBusschere and Willis Reed, expert defensive players, managed to keep the Milwaukee offense off balance and unable to score. When the final buzzer sounded, the Knicks had won. During those five minutes, they scored eighteen points while Milwaukee failed to make a single point! And why had they won? Of course talent and hard work had a lot to do with it. But most importantly, they'd never stopped hoping. They had refused to be quick quitters.

Admittedly, keeping hope alive and refusing to be a quick quitter does not always bring victory, but it does shift the odds in your favor. The score would have been altogether different if the Knicks had said, "Oh, there's no way we can win. Forget it. Let's just save our energy." Hope is a vitalizer. It helps make good things happen.

I'm always lifted up and inspired whenever I think of an incident which occurred during the early days of World War II, when England was experiencing one of her darkest hours. Prime Minister Winston Churchill had just presented a bleak account of the country's state to its leaders. Things looked bad for England. Then Churchill said, "Gentlemen, the situation is grave, but I find it rather inspiring." He knew that even though there was the possibility of imminent defeat, hope would breed courage—the courage to keep on trying. He knew that England could not possibly win unless she kept hoping and kept trying for victory.

A physician friend once told me about a wise bit of counsel he had received from a teacher while in medical school. The teacher was a deeply sensitive and spiritual man as well as an excellent physician. "There will be many times in your career when you will work with a patient for whom nothing more can be done," the teacher said. "Death will seem inevitable. You will be tempted to give up hope. But remember this. Never give up hope ahead of the patient." Later, when working at his own medical practice and encountering instances when a patient seemed on the verge of death, my physician friend remembered that teacher's advice, doubled his efforts and saw many patients take miraculous turns toward life and health.

Several years ago, Len Moreland, a member of Marble Collegiate Church, lay critically ill in a hospital while his wife, Grace, sat nearby. Len's physician arrived and summoned Grace into the hallway. "I have some bad news for you, Grace," he said. "Things are not going well at all. It's not likely that Len will live through the night."

Tears came, but Grace fought to control her emotions. She returned to the room where Len lay unconscious. She couldn't give up hope. And she couldn't stand by, helpless. "What can I do to help?" she asked earnestly.

Then, as if in answer to her question, a passage from the Bible came to her mind: "Is any among you sick? Let him call for the elders of the church, and let them pray over him, anointing him with oil in the name of the Lord; and the prayer of faith will save the sick man, and the Lord will raise him up. . . ." (James 5:14-15)

Grace didn't have time to call the elders. Len needed help right then. She would have to stand in for the elders. She looked around the room for some oil. There was none. But there was a small cup of glycerine and lemon juice which a nurse had prepared earlier for Len's fever-parched lips. It would have to suffice. Grace poured some of it into her hand and put it on Len's hot forehead while she prayed aloud that God would heal him. She hoped that although he was unconscious, Len could still hear her words.

All through the long hours of the night Grace stayed at Len's side. Between moments of prayer she tried to keep her anxious mind occupied by reading some of the magazines left in the room, but no words could penetrate her thoughts. Then she took a Bible, opened it at random and found herself in the Psalms. As she said later, "All of a sudden I was no longer just seeing words. These words had meaning and power. I read the Twenty-Third Psalm. The fourth verse, "Though I walk through the valley of the shadow of death, I will fear no evil," "gave me instant comfort. I was no longer afraid."

"I kept thumbing through the Bible and it seemed there was something for me on every page I turned to. The Holy Spirit must have been directing my fingers. The scripture was strengthening my prayers for my husband."

As the soft light of dawn drifted through the curtains of the hospital room, Grace noticed that Len's breathing seemed easier and more regular. She touched his forehead. It was cool. Len had passed through the crisis and the healing process had begun. Later in the day Len and Grace discussed the events of the night. As Grace told about putting oil on Len's forehead, she asked, "Did you hear my prayer?"

"I certainly did," he told her. "And it helped me to want to live."

Was it a miracle? I think so. But miracles never come to the quick quitters. Miracles, including the miracle of growth, belong to those who keep on hoping.

Part 3

How To Grow Spirituality

Now faith is the substance of things hoped for, the evidence of things not seen.

Hebrews 11:1

INTRODUCTION

During my last year at the Union Theological Seminary in New York City, I took a course in preaching taught by the late Robert McCracken who was then pastor of New York's Riverside Church. Dr. McCracken, successor to Harry Emerson Fosdick, was respected and loved as a great Christian leader and an excellent preacher. It was his custom to have a conference with each student after the student delivered his final sermon and it was with great trepidation that I went to his office one day for that purpose. In seminary, much emphasis was placed upon the importance of theologically accurate sermons and I was still struggling with my theology.

Conversely, most of the other students seemed to have a well-organized theology that they could articulate. All I could say was that Jesus is central in my life and there's something real to faith, and that was about it. After four

77

years of college and three years of seminary, that didn't seem very much. Knowing Dr. McCracken to be quite an intellectual, I felt it would be wise to tell the simple truth, to confess my lack and let the chips fall where they might.

"Dr. McCracken," I confessed forthrightly, "I haven't worked out my theology yet."

His reply surprised me. "Arthur, you're fortunate," he said quietly. "That means you're not locked into any system of thinking which, at this stage of life, probably wouldn't be your own, anyway. You have the rest of your life to grow spiritually."

Doctor McCracken never knew what he did for me that day. I left his office greatly encouraged and relieved. I had learned from him that it was not only permissible but indeed preferable not to have a theology worked out prematurely. I felt free to explore further.

I looked forward to this continuing search with a sense that sometime very soon I would know more fully than ever before how Jesus turns people on to life—that it would happen to me. I had had mere glimpses of Jesus' power, but I needed and wanted more.

Less than a month after my session with Dr. McCracken, I spent an afternoon visiting with my friend Mary Brinig. Mary and her husband, Harold, were directors of the young adult group at Marble Collegiate Church. Mary, a deeply committed Christian, understands from her own experience how greatly a person's life changes when he becomes totally committed to Jesus. For two wonderful hours, I listened to Mary tell story after story about how God so often takes an ordinary life and with it does extraordinary things.

After leaving Mary's apartment that day, I walked slowly up Park Avenue knowing that something wonderful had happened to me, knowing that life and my ministry would now have the vitality and power she described.

The path growth takes is rarely plain and straight, and my spiritual growth was no exception. After experiencing the exhilaration of Mary's testimony I went through a psychological phase, studying the relationship between religion and psychology. For a time I thought psychology was the way to Christian growth. After that I went through a social-action phase during which I thought the answers were surely to be found in social programs. What great trials congregations must suffer in the growth meanderings of their pastors! God must have a special reward for the people who remain patient and enduring while their young pastors grow up spiritually.

"God can take an ordinary life," Mary Brinig had said, "and with it do extraordinary things." That one, plain statement somehow stayed with me. As I pondered it, the simple and yet profound meaning of it gradually dawned on me and I came to realize that the real and only energy for spiritual and personal growth comes from a total commitment of one's life to Jesus Christ. In Christ there is the power for the abundant life—the victorious, overcoming life—which He alone can give and which He came to bring. When the Lord of Creation saved man from sin and death, He saved him from a number of other things as well. Jesus saved us from doubt and fear and desperation, from loneliness and bondage and insecurity and defeat. *To as many as believe on His Name*, the Bible tells us, *He gives power to become the sons of God.* He sets us free. Free to live a victorious life, here and now, no matter what our circumstances. Free forever, because when we become the sons of God, we are His children throughout eternity. No amount of psychology or philosophy or social action can ever substitute for what God alone can give us in reconciling us to Himself through His Son. The life of victory, peace and joy begins with the Atonement. Growth comes later. Real growth begins after birth—after spiritual rebirth.

CHAPTER 13

Faith: Miracle Material

ONE OF THE MOST INCREDIBLE—and encouraging—statements in the Bible is recorded in John 14:12 where Jesus said, "He who believes in me will also do the works that I do; and greater works than these will he do." This remarkable promise says that the power available to Jesus is also available to you and to me. This power is ours when our need is sufficient and our faith strong enough to let it work through us.

For several years my wife and I provided for European girls the experience of living here in America. Early one winter morning as I approached my office I saw Josianne, a young French girl who was spending a year with us, sitting by the door with her head bowed as if she were praying. I was surprised to see her because I thought she was not to return from her trip to Canada until the next day.

"Josianne, you're back early," I said. "Welcome home."

She looked up, and instead of the usual rosy smile, I

saw a pale, drawn face surrounded by a cloud of auburn hair.

"My purse was stolen at the Port Authority bus station," she replied dismally.

Being a New Yorker, my first reaction was to tell her that she could forget about ever seeing her purse again. Such things do not happen in New York. But Josianne stopped me before I could say a word.

"Oh, but I'm praying I'll get it back," she said confidently.

I knew Josianne well, and I knew she had an uncanny ability to accomplish the unlikely. I remembered the many times I had seen her reading the Bible in order to grow in faith and then using her faith to solve problems. At one time she had wanted to go to a Bible college. She had no money and college seemed impossible. But she prayed, read her Bible and believed something would happen—and it did. Someone gave her the money for tuition. On another occasion she had wanted to go to a Christian conference in Dallas, Texas, almost two thousand miles away. That, too, seemed impossible; yet she confidently announced that God would provide a way and He did. She went to the conference, too.

Yet, as we talked about the purse, I kept telling Josianne how unlikely it was to be returned. Josianne said she wanted to pray some more about the problem and asked if I would then take her to the Port Authority terminal. I agreed.

When we arrived at the police station in the terminal, I first introduced myself and then Josianne. Then, before I could say another word the officer behind the desk announced, "I've been trying to get you people on the phone." He held the phone away from his ear and said, "In fact, your phone is ringing right now. We have this young lady's purse."

He put down the phone, and I stood there with my mouth hanging open, speechless.

Josianne seemed not to be surprised at all. She looked first at me and then at the officer. At last a smile broke out across her face.

"Josianne, do you know how unusual this is?" I asked.

"Yes, but I prayed. And I believed I would get it back," she said.

It all seemed very natural and predictable to Josianne. She was a person who knew the power of faith. She'd had a need, and as usual, she'd let her faith work for her. Not everything turned out so well for her, but something significant always happened. She simply dared to believe. She had the kind of faith Charles Kingsley, a nineteenth century English clergyman, novelist and poet, described when he wrote, "I do not merely want to possess a faith; I want a faith to possess me."

Dick Olsen, a handsome young advertising executive, experienced the power of faith in an even more dramatic way. Dick was invited one day by his friend, Jack McMasters, a seventeen-year veteran pilot, to ride in Jack's new airplane.

The flight began in an ordinary way at New York's busy LaGuardia Airport. With full fuel tanks Jack and Dick made their way to the runway, waited for the signal from the control tower and started their takeoff. They were about half way down the runway when they heard the loud, harsh sound of metal hitting the pavement. Then, as they left the ground, there was a noise that sounded like bullets hitting the plane. The plane began to fall and then, with the loud sound of metal hitting cement, they feebly catapulted into the air. The craft shivered and thundered as Jack fought to keep it from crashing.

"Can we circle so we can land?" Dick thought desperately as cold pangs of fear gripped him. He looked at Jack, whose intense, determined face was intent on the controls as he worked feverishly to stay in the air.

Then Dick noticed something reassuring about Jack's expression. "I had faith in Jack's skill as a pilot," Dick said later. "But I also thought about his devout faith in God and the fact that he went to Mass every day. Though I was not a believer, at that moment, I actually found myself having faith in *Jack's faith*."

Jack leaned over and called to the control tower in a matter-of-fact voice, "This is N9JC. I have a problem," he said tersely.

Dick, also a pilot, could not restrain himself. "We don't have a problem," he interrupted loudly. "We have an emergency!"

The men in the control tower were watching the plane. They knew there was an emergency and had dispatched emergency vehicles to the spot where they thought the plane would come down.

Dick stared as the red lights flashed beneath him. *Those guys in the trucks can help down there. But they can't do a thing for us up here!* he thought.

Then another sight caught Dick's attention. Overhead, the giant passenger jets circling the airport in the familiar rhythmic landing patterns were beginning to scatter in all directions. Every pilot in the vicinity knew they were in real trouble, and they were all getting out of Jack's way.

There was not enough time to put foam on the runway before the plane came down. Jack's plane was less than two hundred feet in the air, and it was all he could do to keep it flying. Jack knew if he could not get the landing gear down, he would have to make a belly landing. With fuel tanks full, the plane probably would explode. Still, he had no way of knowing whether the landing gear had dropped into place until he touched ground.

Jack began the descent. The runway rushed straight at them. Suddenly they felt a bump. The landing gear was down! But the plane was still difficult to control, and in seconds it had gone off the end of the runway. Jack finally managed to stop the plane on a grassy spot a short distance beyond the pavement.

When the two men climbed out of the cockpit, they stared in stunned silence. One propeller was broken. Six inches of metal was missing from the tip of each blade. The other propeller was bent into an S-shape. The bending of the propeller must have provided enough force to catapult the plane into the air. The fuselage was filled with holes from bits of asphalt and cement which had been thrown up by the propellers as they hit the runway. Now Dick knew what had caused the bullet-like sounds he'd heard on takeoff.

Dick began to shake. He had known all along they were in trouble, but he hadn't realized how much. They were incredibly fortunate, he felt, to be standing there looking at the plane.

By this time, a crowd of people, including the airport manager, had surrounded the plane. "I thought you fellows would never make it," the manager said. "Look at this," he went on, pointing to a broken light on the belly of the plane. "If you had dipped another inch, you would have exploded! How in the world did you make it?"

Pale and drained from the experience, Jack wondered if he should try to tell them. There was no doubt about what power had kept them up and brought them down safely. But would the others believe him? Even if they didn't, he had to tell them.

"Do you see the JC in my number?" Jack asked. "That stands for Jesus Christ. Every plane I have ever owned has had those letters on it. I know He's always with me, on every flight."

Stunned men looked at one another, but no one challenged Jack's remarks. Something miraculous had happened they couldn't deny. A plane which could easily have crashed had landed safely and two men who'd been on the brink of death were still alive and safe.

Dick Olsen and Jack McMasters were more than just lucky. No one could ever convince either of them that the outcome of that flight was due to anything less than the presence of Jesus Christ and they knew that they'd experienced another miracle of faith.

The experience helped Jack McMaster's faith grow even stronger. But more importantly, it helped Dick Olsen grow from a man who did not believe in God to one who could not help but believe. When Dick climbed aboard Jack's plane, he was a non-believer. "I didn't believe in God or Jesus or in any of that religious stuff," he said. "But after that ride, it was a different story. It made a believer out of me!"

Faith is the stuff miracles are made of!

CHAPTER 14

The Meaning of Faith

ONE DAY WHEN THINGS were going rather rough for Frank Small, a man whom I consider to be one of the spiritual giants at the Marble Collegiate Church, he uttered in my presence a phrase he had learned from his childhood on a Mississippi farm where he'd spent much time with his grandparents. "When there's trouble on earth," he said, "there's lots of motion in heaven."

This was a new expression to me and I wasn't sure of its meaning. But more important to me was how Frank would explain it.

"What does that mean?" I asked.

"Whenever one of us is in trouble," he said, "God gets himself in motion to help. It's that simple."

I've often reflected on that bit of wisdom, and I'm always comforted by it. It is reassuring to know that every time I am in difficulty, God gets in motion to help.

Joan Sonntag, one of my fellow workers at the church, knows from experience just what Frank was talking about.

Some time ago, Joan discovered a growth on her back and, after consulting with her physician, was told it might be malignant. The growth was small on the outside but the physician was sure it was much larger on the inside. The surgery, he said, could be serious.

As Joan spoke anxiously about her forthcoming hospitalization she seemed particularly concerned about the kind of room she would have. "I must have a private room," she confided to a friend. "I can't afford it, but I must have one."

"Joan," her friend pleaded, "semi-private rooms aren't bad, and private rooms cost a small fortune nowadays."

"I know they do, but I absolutely can't bear the thought of being in the same situation my father was in a few months ago," Joan said. "He was in the hospital, and the man who occupied the bed next to him was awful. He nagged, complained and demanded so much that he made life miserable for everyone. My father would have recovered much sooner if it hadn't been for that old man." She paused, then added, her voice rising, "I have enough trouble of my own to deal with. I don't need somebody else's problems. I just want to be alone."

When Joan was admitted to the hospital, her worst fears became reality. A private room was not available and she was put into a room with another woman who was critically ill and who looked to be very old. At first Joan was distressed but she felt better when she found that the woman was sweet and gracious and not the least bit demanding.

During her first night in the room Joan was awakened by the half-stifled sobs of the woman in the next bed. She became annoyed. Nevertheless, she got up, talked with her roommate for a moment, adjusted her pillow, and then went back to bed. She had not been asleep long when she was awakened again. This time the crying was louder and more uncontrollable.

"I can't stand it! I can't stand it!" the woman cried.

Joan went to the woman's bedside. "Are you hurting badly? Is there anything I can do?" Joan asked.

'Oh, I'm so sorry to disturb you, but the pain is unbearable and nothing relieves it," the woman sobbed. "I don't know how much longer I can stand it."

Joan pulled a chair close to the woman's bed, sat down and took her hand. She sat there for a while holding the thin hand and talking softly until the woman appeared to be a little more relaxed. Finally her roommate dozed off and Joan climbed back into her own bed.

The next morning after breakfast Joan got out her cassette tape player and began to listen to a tape by Nell Martin, a Christian laywoman who was telling about her relationship with Christ and how he loves all people. Joan was trying to find spiritual strength in those words. Surgery was drawing closer, and she was afraid.

While listening to the tape, Joan noticed that her roommate seemed to be listening, too. "Would you like to hear this?" she asked. The woman nodded yes, and Joan turned up the volume.

When the tape was finished, Joan looked to her rooommate for a response. The woman was unusually still. Joan looked more closely—then suddenly realized the woman was dead. She had died listening to Nell Martin tell about how much Jesus loved her.

When I spoke with Joan later about the incident, she said emphatically, "I was supposed to be in that room. I didn't know it at first, but I was put there for a purpose. It was hard to get up at night when the woman cried, but it helped me to get outside of myself and to minister to somebody whose need was much greater than mine."

Then Joan spoke of the loneliness and selfishness of pain. "When we're in pain as I was, everything is drawn to us, and we think we're the only ones in the world," she said. "But we're not. Being with that woman as she suffered and died helped me get a much better perspective about myself."

Many of us are like Joan. We may not know when God has a special use for us. When she was placed in that room, Joan didn't know it, but she had a hidden treasure which God could use at the right time in the right place. She had a faith to share that was bigger than she thought.

Joan experienced that day the truth of Paul's words to the Romans: "All things work together for good to them that love God..." And she learned that trusting in God meant allowing Him the opportunity to use her to help someone else. God was in motion that day for Joan and through her for someone else.

We never know when or how or under what circumstances God will speak to us. But we don't need to know. We need only to be aware that God is constantly desiring to say something to us and through us, if we will but listen.

The ultimate expression of the deep, penetrating meaning that faith can give to a person's life is demonstrated in the story of a young girl whose name may never be known. She died in a Nazi concentration camp during World War II. But her faith will never be forgotten. On the wall of the cell she occupied until her death, an Allied soldier found these words which she had written:

> *I believe in the sun*
> *Even when it is not shining:*
> *I believe in love*
> *Even when feeling it not.*
> *I believe in God,*
> *Even when He is silent.*

Such faith doesn't come easy. But we can have it if we take God as our partner and trust Him, giving Him a chance to bring good out of every tough situation we face. If we will do this we will grow in experience and in faith.

CHAPTER 15

The Power of Faith

IF MORE PEOPLE REALIZED what faith can do for them, they would be eager to have more of it. Faith has incredible power. Leo Tolstoy, the famous Russian novelist, discovered the power of faith and described it as a force of life. Tolstoy discovered that faith is a tremendous force which can transform life from the ordinary to the extraordinary. Its energy emanates from God—and when it is released, the power of faith becomes one of the greatest powers in the world. Faith power is God power.

Faith in God makes people greater than any problem. Faith is powerful enough to stop the mouths of hungry lions, to enable man to stand against the onslaught of insurmountable problems, even death.

I am inspired and motivated every time I read from Hebrews (10:39) "We are not those who shrink back and are destroyed but of those who have faith and keep their souls." We are encouraged to develop a strong, enduring faith and in so doing we gain the resource needed to overcome any problem.

No one knows the power of faith better than Christiane Tuchel, an exchange visitor from Germany who lived with my family during her one year spent in America. A tall, pretty, blue-eyed blonde, Christiane is a resourceful and intelligent woman in her early twenties. During her visit, she wanted to see as much of this country as she could, and she did. Every Sunday she would spend the afternoon exploring New York City. She walked hundreds of miles through Manhattan, Brooklyn and Queens. It was a good thing for her that she never told us in advance about those sightseeing expeditions. My wife and I would have discouraged her for these excursions sometimes took her to parts of the city where young women just don't walk alone.

One of Christiane's goals was to visit every one of the forty-eight contiguous states. Before her summer vacation began she had already visited sixteen and she planned to see the others. She bought a thirty-day bus pass and drew up an itinerary which would take her thousands of miles around the country, from New England to the Pacific Northwest to the gulf coast and the southern states.

As the day of departure drew near, Gloria began to worry. "Art," she said, "we can't let her go so far alone. Something will happen to her. She's too young for such a trip."

"Don't worry about Christiane," I told her. "She's resourceful. She can take care of herself. She'll be all right."

My prediction was only partly true. Christiane was fine until she arrived in Oklahoma City early on a Sunday morning after an all-night trip. There she discovered she had a three-hour layover. Christiane then did what she usually did when she had time to spend in a new place. She began to walk.

After a while, she realized she was not going in the direction she had intended to go, so she walked up to a young man standing on a nearby corner and asked him for directions. To her surprise, he offered to walk with her.

Christiane was not sure that was such a good idea but she took a close look at him. He was clean-shaven, presentable. He wore neatly pressed slacks and a stylish, open-collared sport shirt, and was neat and clean-cut. At last she reluctantly agreed.

After they'd walked for several minutes, Christiane realized she was still not going in the right direction. She and the young man were circling around in a section of town where the houses were becoming father and farther apart. When at last she became aware that they were moving away from the center of the city. Christiane became frightened. She began to wonder if she had misjudged the man. She stole a glance at him. Yes, there was something about him she did not like, something she could not define.

She immediately became cautious about her conversation for fear of antagonizing him and causing additional problems. Frightened, without the slightest idea of where she was, accompanied by a suspicious stranger, Christiane grew desperate.

"Let's go this way," she said timidly to the man and pointed in a different direction.

"We're going this way," he said firmly, narrowing his eyes and looking fiercely at her. She could feel her knees getting weak, as fear gripped her. "No," she insisted as she turned to walk away from him. "I want to go this way."

"Oh, no you don't," he snapped as he put his hand into his pocket and suddenly drew out a knife. "We're going this way, and you had better do exactly as I say if you don't want to get hurt."

Christiane froze.

"Move," he said as he gave her a push and slid the

open knife up his sleeve so that it could not be seen. They started walking again, as he fell in a few steps to the side and slightly behind her, watching her every move.

After what seemed an eternity, they came to a secluded spot where at last he grabbed her arm. Christiane screamed loudly but there was no one to hear. She struggled, hitting and kicking as hard as she could. But he was strong and much bigger than she was. She felt herself becoming weak. Suddenly the man grabbed her throat and began to squeeze with both hands.

"Dear God, help me!" Christiane prayed. "He's going to kill me. What can I do? Please God, save me!"

Swift as a dart, this thought came suddenly to mind: "One with God is a majority." What a time, she thought, to be recalling a quote she had heard in a sermon! She needed real help, not a sermon. But, she thought then, this was not a random quote. There was a message. God was telling her something.

"Christiane, you and I are a majority. Stop struggling and listen to me. I will help you," she heard the inner voice say.

She went limp. She stopped struggling and tried with all her might to yield to the power of God. As she let her hands fall to her side, she looked the man straight in the eye. He was so surprised that he loosened his grip on her throat. Christiane took a deep breath.

"It's Sunday morning," she said quietly "and I'm praying for you, that you will be all right. You know, God loves you," she went on in a voice so calm it surprised her. Her words also surprised her assailant. Where had those words come from? A few seconds earlier she had been screaming in fear, and now she was telling her assailant she was praying for him.

Those weren't my words, she thought. *Those were God's words,* and they are the help I need. God's message seemed suddenly to reach the man. He dropped his hands and stood staring at her.

"You walk that way," Christiane said with quiet authority pointing in the opposite direction from where they'd come. "I'll get back to town by myself. I won't tell anyone about this."

The man continued to stare at her, looking puzzled, as if he could not believe what he had heard. He started to say something, then stopped, turned abruptly and walked away. Christiane walked quickly back toward town, never turning to look back.

When she got back to the bus station, the shock of what had happened struck her. For a moment she began to shake and cry, then again felt a strange calmness. She had been on the brink of death, she realized, but had escaped.

And she knew why. The scriptures say, ". . . though I walk through the valley of the shadow of death, I will fear no evil for Thou art with me." Christiane had believed the truth of that reassuring psalm and although the odds seemed completely against her and she had been overwhelmed by fear, she had nevertheless determined to listen to God's Voice. She had heard Him say, "You and I are a majority," and from those words had grown the courage she needed to handle her situation. No problem would even be so big that she and God could not handle it together.

What Christiane discovered is true for everyone. God wants to do something great for each of us. And to demonstrate His desire He gives anyone who will accept it a faith big enough to meet any situation. We need only to call on Him when we have a problem, asking Him for help. Then believing we will receive, we reach out to Him and accept the power. The greatest power in the universe—the power of faith.

CHAPTER 16

The Value of Proper Prayer

A PSYCHOLOGIST FRIEND who is a Christian asked me one day what I thought was one of the greatest and at the same time most therapeutic experiences a human being could have. It was obvious by the way he asked the question that he had the answer on the tip of his tongue and was more eager to tell me what he thought than to hear what I thought. So I gave him the opportunity.

"What is it?" I asked. "You tell me."

"Prayer," he replied, "meditative prayer."

His answer excited me. Here was an expert in human behavior telling a minister that nothing is greater or more helpful to a person than prayer. I wanted to hear more.

"Tell me what you mean by meditative prayer." I said.

"I can only tell you the way I experience it," he explained.

I have never studied meditation or even read much

about it. But several years ago I fell into a habit of praying which has done me more good than I can say."

"Tell me about it," I ventured.

"Frequently, before I go to bed at night," he went on, "after my family is asleep and everything is quiet, I will sit in my living room, get loose, get as relaxed as I can, and focus my mind on God. Sometimes all I will do is keep the word God in my mind. At other times I will pray for whatever persons or concerns come to mind. But those moments of quiet prayer have an incredible effect on me. I experience a great sense of peace and feel such love around me. I feel as if I am in harmony with all creation. Do you know what I'm talking about?"

"Yes, I do." I agreed. "I often do the same thing and have the same experience as you have described. From these experiences I know what the hymn writer meant when he wrote the lyrics to the hymn, "Sweet Hour of Prayer." Those moments are sweet and beautiful. Then, as an after thought, I added, "Its great for relieving tension, isn't it?" My friend confessed that it was his tension that got him started with it in the first place. I admitted the same was true of myself.

It's usually some kind of need or crisis that motivates us to pray at all. That's the way God works things. If we had everything solved and were functioning perfectly, we wouldn't need God. And it's obvious from what the scriptures say and what life tells us that God wants us to need Him. But what about the many times we go to him praying sincerely for an answer that things don't come out right, especially when the right answer seems obvious to us? A woman who had been struggling with that problem for sometime told me about what happened when she changed the focus of her prayer.

"I had been praying the wrong prayer for many years," she said. "But when I changed my prayer, my world began to change. I'm married to a very good man who is faithful, provides well and is always around. Basically everything about him is all right except for the fact that he's such a grouch. He's often selfish and demanding. Rarely does he ever compliment me. He seems to grump and growl most of the time. For years," she continued, "I prayed that my husband would become kinder, nicer and gentler, but for some reason that prayer wasn't answered. Then one Sunday morning while I was in church you prayed something like this in your pastoral prayer: *Dear Lord, help us to be loving to those who are unloving, kind to the unkind and sweet to the sour.* When you said that, I had a revelation about myself instead of for him. I prayed for strength to work on myself so that I could be kind and gentle even when he wasn't.

"I started reacting differently to my husband," she said. "I stopped growling every time he did. Only a few days passed before I noticed a change beginning to take place in him. He's not every thing I would like him to be now, but he's a whole lot better."

I imagine every one of us is praying for something which at this moment is difficult and complicated, and for some reason the answer isn't coming. Perhaps you're asking yourself, "How long will I have to wait? How much more frustration and disillusionment will I have to take before this prayer is answered?" Well, I don't know how long you may have to wait for the answer, but I do know you may not have to wait too long if you have help. Where, then, can you go for help?

In my opinion, the best help comes from the scriptures, especially Paul's letter to the Romans. "Likewise the Spirit helps us in our weakness; for we do not know how to pray as we ought, but the Sprit himself intercedes for us with signs too deep for words." (Romans 8:26) With some interpretation of my own, this is what Paul said: We don't know how to pray as we ought. In fact, much of the time we're relatively weak in our prayer life, but that doesn't mean we should stop praying. The thing to do is to keep on praying with a mind open to the presence of the Spirit. When the mind is open to His presence, the Spirit begins to intercede. He gets inside and begins to pray on our behalf. And when that happens, dramatic changes take place.

If you're praying about something in particular, keep on praying. If you want something you think is right, keep praying persistently for it, and as you pray keep your mind open to the movement of the Holy Spirit who will in His own time begin to pray for you and correct the course of your prayer if that is what is needed.

Louis Evely, a Belgian priest, wrote something about prayer which has been most helpful to me. He said, "Praying means surrendering to the influence of the Holy Spirit, becoming calm and collected, so that we may grow docile as He prays in us. . . ."

Docile is an interesting word. It means being capable of being taught, willing to receive training, teachable. When you pray, get calm and collected and be docile, preparing the way for the Spirit to pray on your behalf.

Wasn't that the way Jesus prayed? Jesus was a strong-minded individual, much stronger than any of us. He had human desires, yet before His Father, He was docile. Perhaps the greatest illustration of this took place in Gethsemane the night He was betrayed.

Jesus knew His time was almost up and He would die a painful, humiliating death. Nothing could have been worse. Jesus didn't want to die and so He began to pray, "My Father, if it be possible, let this cup pass from me. . . ." Only a few recorded words of Jesus' prayers that night remain, but He must have prayed a very long time. The prayer which began with His wish ended with "nevertheless, not as I will, but as thou wilt." (Matthew 26:39). The Holy Spirit had interceded and was praying on

His behalf. Nothing can be greater for you and me than to learn as Jesus did to pray the right prayer for ourselves in the power of the Holy Spirit.

Many years ago my wife, Gloria, prayed unsuccessfully for the solution to a special problem. When the answer was not forthcoming, instead of persisting and adjusting her prayer, she gave up the prayer and with it her attempt to solve the problem. She stopped until a few years ago when fear, embarrassment and disgust motivated her into another attempt at a solution.

It was on a beautiful summer day when Gloria, our two sons Paul and Chuck and I walked among the remains of the ancient Incan city of Machu Picchu, perched high atop a mountain peak in the Andes in Peru. To reach the city, one must take a bus from the train station in the valley at the base of the mountain, then go along a dirt road which makes seventeen hairpin curves in its steep ascent. As we climbed, we were awed by the genius of the natives who had built such a fortress of enormous granite blocks and made gentle terraces from such rugged terrain. Those ancient builders had worked without the conveniences of modern equipment. And they'd built around all the disadvantages of the location—sheer cliffs dropping straight to the jungle floor hundreds of feet below.

At one point we had to climb stone steps along the edge of a precipice and there was no guard rail. I was walking ahead, and when I turned to speak to Gloria I discovered she was not behind me. In a moment I saw her clinging fearfully to the inner wall at the top of the stone steps, her face pale with fright. An old terror of heights, which she had never mentioned and had managed to hide by avoiding high places, had suddenly seized her.

Ten-year-old Chuck, standing nearby, offered to help his mother either walk to where I was or return to the terrace below, but Gloria could not stand up. Her legs were like rubber and her heart was racing madly.

"Oh, I feel like an idiot!" she said helplessly. "I know this is silly, but I can't help myself. I can't climb any further. Just leave me alone, and I'll crawl back down the steps to the terrace."

And that is exactly what she did. She retreated on all fours! It was a terrifying and humiliating experience for Gloria, especially as our two young sons stood by seeing their mother immobilized with fear.

On that day Gloria resolved to overcome her fear of heights. This time she would start praying for help and stick to her prayers. And she would believe that God would help her to conquer her horrible fear.

The following summer in Rome we were about to climb into the dome of St. Peter's Basilica. Our guide told us that the passage to the top was a curved staircase with three hundred steps and explained that once we started up we could not change our minds and come down. We had to go all the way to the top in order to get back down. Hesitant, I turned to Gloria and said, "Are you really sure you want to tackle this one?"

"I must," she replied resolutely, remembering all the praying she had done since the experience in Peru. "I have to face the thing I fear if I'm ever going to conquer it. Besides, if all of the people who climb this dome every day can make it to the top and down again, I can too."

As we started out, Gloria decided to count the steps to keep her mind occupied so she would not think about the height. But at the sixtieth step she froze. "I can't move," she said, trembling.

"Maybe we can squeeze our way back down the stairs," I suggested. "I'm sure the people behind us will understand."

101

"No, I can't go back," she protested. "I've got to go all the way to the top. I can't back down now. Just keep going by yourselves, and I'll meet you at the top."

I wanted to stay and help her, but I realized she had to get through the experience by herself. The boys and I continued to climb.

"Sixty-one, sixty-two," she counted as she climbed slowly. As step number seventy a group of people reached her and stopped.

"Are you all right?" one man asked.

"Just a little tired, I guess," she said. "Please try to squeeze past me." She pressed her body close to the smooth stone wall. They went past but fear was overwhelming her. She could not move.

"What if more people come and can't get by because I'm blocking them? What will I do then? What if I can't climb any more and can't get down either?" she cried. "Oh, I've got to get out of here!"

Then she realized what was happening to her. "Dear Lord," she prayed, "don't let me panic or I'll never make it." She started to climb again.

About twenty minutes later, Gloria emerged from the stairwell and stood clinging to the doorway. A cool breeze hit her face as she breathed deeply. "Oh, Art, I made it!" she said, relieved. Her face was pale and she was trembling. Silently she thanked God, who had been her silent partner in the climb.

"Stay right there," I told her. "Don't come over here near the rail. It's a long way down."

"I've got to," she argued. "I have to look all the way down to the bottom, and then I'll be all right." With those words, she walked to the rail and, clenching it so tightly her knuckles blanched, she forced herself to look down. "I made it. I really made it!" she exclaimed. Then she stood silent for a moment.

"It's beautiful," she said as she looked out across the city. "Rome is beautiful. And I would have missed all this if I hadn't forced myself to climb to the top. I've really conquered my fear this time, Art. I'm shaky, but I'm not afraid."

She had licked it—and in so doing had grown bigger than her fear.

The key to Gloria's success was prayer and the belief that God would help her solve her problem if she prayed the right prayer and didn't give up. And it worked.

CHAPTER 17

Alone with God

THERE'S A COMMON MALADY prevalent in the 20th century which we might call the "rushing" syndrome. We rush to work. We rush home. We even rush to stop rushing. But we don't stop until we have a full-blown case of the rushing syndrome. Something is wrong and we know it. The symptoms are a sense of futility and dissatisfaction, worry and fatigue due to overwork in trying to get somewhere fast without a clear set of directions. The person who has the malady knows he wants to go somewhere, to make a constructive contribution to life, but he's so busy rushing that he doesn't take the time to evaluate his progress.

There's a cure for that malady which is exceptionally effective. The answer is found in these words from the French mathematician and philosopher of the 17th century, Blaise Pascal: "All men's miseries come from their inability to sit quietly and alone."

The cure for the rushing syndrome is the quiet time.

In Hamlet, William Shakespeare had one of his characters speak these great words of wisdom: "This above all, to thine own self be true." It was another way of saying, "You must grow in the direction and with the rhythm which is best for you." But to do so you must attain a perspective concerning yourself. No one can really know himself and judge whether he is being true to himself unless he first gets quiet and thinks things through.

Some of the most influential personalities of all times, Socrates, Confucius, St. Francis and many others, were people who knew the value of getting alone and becoming quiet in order to think, pray and meditate. They knew that such a quiet time was absolutely essential to achieving their right objectives. Even Jesus did this.

A successful, high-powered business executive, president of his own firm, once told me about why he spends thirty to forty-five minutes each day alone in his office in complete quiet. A few years after he had come to New York he returned for a visit to the Indiana farm where his parents lived. Proud of his business success, he told his parents about his great responsibilities and his demanding, busy schedule. After listening to her son, his mother finally said to him, "Describe a typical day to me."

Her son told her how he got up early every morning, commuted to the city from his home in the suburbs, spent long hours in conferences, luncheon meetings, dinner meetings, and on the telephone.

At last his mother replied, "That's wonderful, son. I'm impressed. But tell me, when do you *think*? When do you think about—God? When do you share your thoughts with Him?"

The son couldn't answer her. He knew that his clever and resourceful thinking had made him successful. But he knew, too, that he was spending all of his time in activities which did not allow him an opportunity to really contemplate his life. He was not taking the time to get a true perspective about himself. That sudden realization shook him because he was smart enough to know what happens to people who don't get the right perspective on themselves.

Just then he decided to schedule a quiet time into every working day. To make it as effective as possible, he scheduled it in the morning. And now his daily schedule includes a quiet time during which no calls or visitors are accepted. After that he schedules the activities which his business requires.

When I asked this man how his daily time alone had affected him, he replied, "I've obviously calmed down a lot. The pressures are there but they don't affect me as much. I feel calm inside," he said, pointing to his heart. "Business problems don't get me down like they used to. But the greatest benefit is that in my quiet time I have come to know God better. I'd been so busy rushing around that I'd begun to lose contact with Him. I'm in touch with God again and I feel I'm doing a better job with my life."

Jesus gave some specific instructions about the quiet time. He directed us to go into the prayer closet and shut the door, getting alone with God and shutting out all distractions. At times, Jesus would go into the hills or down by the seashore alone. There He would pray and meditate on the purpose and direction of His life.

Silence is essential. "The voice of God is a gentle voice," Evelyn Underhill wrote, "and we can't hear it when it is in competition with other voices." The psalmist expressed it in another way: "Be still and know that I am God." (Psalm 46:10) We think, hear and sense best when we learn to be still.

Admiral Richard Byrd, the polar explorer, beautifully

described an experience he had at the South Pole. I recommend that you read it slowly and thoughtfully:

"I paused to listen to the silence. My breath crystallized as it passed my cheeks. Drifted on a breeze gentler than a whisper. My frozen breath hung like a cloud overhead. The day was dying, the night was being born, but with great peace. And here were the imponderable processes and forces of the cosmos, harmonious and soundless. Harmony, that it was. That was what came out of the silence. A gentle rhythm. The train of a perfect chord. The music of the spheres, perhaps. It was enough to catch that rhythm momentarily to be myself a part of it. In that instant, I could feel no doubt of man's oneness with the universe, and the conviction came that that rhythm was too orderly, too harmonious, too perfect to be a product of blind chance. That there must be a purpose in the whole and that man was part of the whole and not an accidental offshoot. It was a feeling that transcended reason, that went to the heart of man's despair and found it groundless. The universe was a cosmos, not a chaos. Man was rightfully a part of that cosmos as were the day and night."

Moments of solitude can constitute some of the greatest time we have, but we must be ready to take full advantage of what they can offer. We must anticipate the good which comes from being creatively alone.

One July morning I got up before the sun, climbed on my bicycle and rode to a small cove on the opposite side of the Maine island where my family and I spend each summer. I settled myself on a huge granite boulder to await the sunrise. I knew it wouldn't take long, for shades of pink rapidly turned to red on the eastern horizon. As I waited, the air was nippy; the chill of night still in it. There were a few disjointed sounds — the waves breaking upon the rocks, some redwing blackbirds beginning to stir in the cattails behind me and a lobsterman out of sight around the cove, banging his traps as he loaded them with bait.

I breathed deeply of the fresh salt air and reveled in the surge of energy it produced. I was completely alone, loving it. The worries and problems of the world seemed far away, and any thought except a pleasant one seemed an alien intruder upon my tranquility. I was at peace with myself and with my world.

Soon the first rays of sun slipped over the ocean's edge and the whole glorious scene before me began to change. A new day was born, and I was refreshed. The night's sleep had restored my body and these few moments of solitude had refreshed my soul. I was ready to face the day and all it held in store. I was prepared to grow with the challenges of the day.

"I never found the companion who was so companionable as solitude," wrote Henry David Thoreau. And I know just what he meant. The ideal companion is like the gentle spring rains which nourish and refresh us, one who brings out the best in us while helping us to grow. All of this and more, time alone can do for us. Why should we fear solitude when we can make of it a friend? It can become our incubator for growth and a refuge from the storms of life.

PART 4

How to Have Better Personal Relationships

And this commandment have we from him,
that he who loveth God love his brother also.
I John 4:21

INTRODUCTION

The week before I was married, I met a woman on the street who'd belonged to the church where I worked while in graduate school. I knew little about her except that she was prominent in civic activities in Houston, Texas, where I lived at the time. We nodded as we approached each other and then, almost as if by prearranged command, stopped to talk. It was the only conversation we had ever had, but it was one of the most important talks I've had with anyone. I believe that God, in His mysterious way, must have arranged it.

"I understand congratulations are in order for you," she said. "Aren't you going to be married next week?"

"Yes, I am," I said, smiling back at her. "Thank you."

"I understand you're marrying a girl from Louisiana," she went on. "I wish you both much happiness."

'Oh, I'm sure we'll be *very* happy," I said confidently.

The lady looked right into my eyes for a few moments, correctly assessing my naiveté and my fatuous assumption that everything would always be great once I was married. There would be no problems. How could there be? My future wife and I loved each other too much to entertain the thought of *problems*. I would learn in time that mine was a common, but totally unrealistic outlook.

"Would you mind if I shared with you something which has been very important in my marriage?" she asked.

"Not at all," I answered, my curiosity aroused.

"I have been married for thirty-seven years, happily so," she said. "I have long since discovered something important. Every day I must work at my marriage, even after all these years. Any day I don't work at it I am taking my husband for granted and that hurts both of us. The same is true of him. When he doesn't work at our marriage, he takes me for granted and we both are shortchanged. I feel it's my business to take 100 percent responsibility for our happiness together. This philosophy has worked for me and explains the success of my marriage."

Her words were convincing. Right away my wife and I started putting her suggestions to work in our marriage, and it's a good thing we did. Gloria and I both have strong personalities, and we've had to make adjustments, especially during the first few years of marriage.

We were helped also by a gem of wise counsel my father offered just moments after he finished performing our wedding ceremony. He pulled us close to each other and to himself and then said, "Just remember this. You are going to get angry with each other. But if you're smart you won't both get angry at the same time."

We laughed then. But we soon discovered how right he was! When we are smart enough to remember his advice, we still save a lot of pain and wasted energy.

Dr. Herbert Manton, a psychiatrist from Cleveland, Ohio, once told me that a good marriage is like a work of art. You love it, shape it and make adjustments so that it will become beautiful. And all this takes time and loving attention. The marriage relationship is the most intimate and demanding one of all, and yet many of the same principles important to a successful marriage are also necessary for success in any other relationship.

I recently read again the Sermon on the Mount, appreciating as never before what Jesus had to say about relationships — with God and with other people. The theme which comes through clearly is that we are to love one another for it is in so doing that we live our love for God. The apostle John was even more direct in stating the necessity of good relationships when he said, "If anyone says he loves God and hates his brother he is a liar; for he who does not love his brother whom he has seen, cannot love God whom he has not seen." (1st John 4:20)

One of the most helpful truths for getting along with others came to me one day while I was listening to someone lecture on the psychology of Alfred Adler. Dr. Adler, Sigmund Freud and Karl Jung were contemporaries and close associates until each went his separate way and developed his own individual theory of human behavior.

The lecture was on sibling relationships and how Adler saw children as affecting one another. Sibling relationships, he thought, sometimes have more effect upon the personality of the child than does the parental relationship. The speaker talked about the interplay between the first and second-born children and how there is frequently much rivalry. As the speaker continued I began to realize how I had related to my older brother. I'd felt I had to compete with him. I'd wanted to go everywhere he went, do everything he did and have everything he had. And he'd always resisted me.

Then the speaker talked about the need, if one wants to be emotionally healthy, to take responsibility for one's own actions and not be dictated to by whatever position he occupied in a relationship. "Stand on your own feet emotionally," he said. "Be in charge of your emotions." The situation itself is not nearly as important as the manner in which we respond to it and what we do with it.

That was a day of awakening for me. I realized fully for the first time that I must take full responsibility for the quality of my relationships, starting with my brother. Since that day he and I have not had a serious disagreement with each other.

People might not always respond to me as I would like, but I can decide how I will respond to them. This is what Jesus spoke about when He preached His most challenging and exciting sermon. I don't always feel like loving others. I don't always feel like being forgiving. It is often easier to judge and often there is an evil pleasure in carrying resentments. Jesus understood these feelings. Yet he also understood the necessity of taking charge of self and rising above them. Jesus spoke directly to each of us when He commanded us to love one another.

I have found that the area of building good relationships is one of enormous potential for personal growth. In addition, it presents a multitude of marvelous opportunities to touch and enhance the lives of others.

CHAPTER 18

The Art of People Building

AFTER MANY YEARS OF SERVICE to mankind Albert Schweitzer wrote: "The only ones among you who will be really happy are those who will have sought and found how to serve." Schweitzer, philosopher, musician, physician and Nobel laureate who achieved fame for his work in Africa, had discovered that the key to happiness is to be the kind of person Jesus spoke of when He said, "He who is greatest among you shall be your servant. . . ." (Matthew 23:11)

When Jesus spoke of the servant, he wasn't talking about lowly positions and menial tasks. He saw the servant's role as the highest because the servant is the person who enables others to enjoy a better life. The servant is a *people builder.* He builds people up instead of tearing them down. He helps others. He learns to heal wounds of body and soul, to turn weakness into strength, to bring out the good qualities in another person. He is the people builder *par excellence,* and he is happy because of it. How, then, is it possible for us to serve others and be people builders?

Every person has a special talent for helping others to grow. You have abilities that are uniquely yours and unlike anyone else's. Each of us must find the right way and the special situations in which to put those unique abilities to work. There is an art to being helpful. There is an art to taking the knowledge and skills you have and matching them effectively to the needs of another person so that person will be helped by your gift.

Few people are more adept in the art of being helpful than a certain man named Angelo. Angelo is the owner and operator of Ardsley Hardware in Ardsley-on-the-Hudson, New York. Angelo is an ordinary man who has found a unique way to help build others—and he does an extraordinary job, thereby making a significant difference in his community.

Not long ago I had a conversation with a former neighbor who had retired and was about to move to another state. "We're going to miss you when you move," I told him.

"I'm really going to miss the hardware store!" he said.

That seemed a strange reply, but as I thought about it, I realized that I might make the same statement if I were about to move. Ardsley Hardware is not just an ordinary hardware store. In fact, the only place I have been which physically resembles it is an old country store on a back road in Vermont. But Angelo's store is on the main street of town and except for its white front you might not even notice it.

Once inside, though, you find yourself in narrow aisles squeezed between big bags of lawn fertilizer, cans of paint, assorted household items and tools. The stock is not spectacular, the prices aren't much better than the store down the road. But almost everyone for miles around goes to Ardsley Hardware.

Why? Because of Angelo. Angelo knows everything there is to know about fixing things around the house and maintaining a lawn. His main purpose in life seems to be to share his knowledge with people who need it. He is a regular storehouse of information. It's not even necessary to know what your problem is to get Angelo's help. Angelo will help you think through a situation, identify the problem and find a solution. He knows when you can do the job yourself and when you're getting in over your head and need a professional. And he's so tactful that it's a rare person who doesn't feel better after just talking with Angelo.

Kids love Angelo, too. One day I watched a boy of about eleven as he walked into the store and up to the counter where Angelo stood. In his mind he must have had a vision of a fantastic go-cart which he was going to build. He didn't have a drawing of it; it was all in his mind. In fact, he didn't even know how to begin, but that fact didn't dampen his enthusiasm. For the next fifteen minutes the boy described his dream project while Angelo listened patiently.

When the boy finished, Angelo said encouragingly, "I know exactly what you have in mind. Let's see if this is what you want." He pulled a rod from under a shelf. "This will do for the axle. The wheels you need aren't in stock, but I can order them. It'll take a couple of days. Can you wait that long?"

The boy nodded. Then the two of them started around the store, collecting nails, screws, braces, all of the things needed to build the go-cart. When they finished, Angelo suddenly asked the boy, "What school do you go to?"

The youth told him, and Angelo replied, nodding,

"Good school. The teachers make you work hard, don't they? Anyone who goes to that school gets a ten percent discount."

As I listened, it was obvious to me that the name of the school didn't matter. It merely gave a legitimate-sounding reason for a discount so that the cost of the cart would be within the boy's budget.

When everything was paid for the boy, grinning with pride and happiness, walked out of the store. Something much greater than merely buying some hardware had taken place. The boy looked as if he felt very good about himself. Not once in their discussion of the project did Angelo look down at the boy or suggest in any way his ideas were unrealistic or his questions ignorant. Angelo simply started where the boy was and helped him work through a problem, building him up instead of tearing him down.

That's creative helping — matching your skills effectively to another person's needs. And it's also the art of people building.

Several summers ago while visiting the village of Weggis, located on a small lake near Lucerne, Switzerland, I met another person who, like Angelo, was effective at people building. Her name is Marijke, and we met while sitting on the wide porch of a hotel, a creamy stucco building with a red tile roof much like the other buildings in the village, and gazing out across the water at the mountains which rose from the opposite shore. It was summertime, so there was no snow on the lower peaks, but in the distance we could see the rugged snow-capped crests of the higher mountains.

After a few minutes the woman, who appeared to be in her early thirties, spoke. "Aren't those mountains beautiful? I come from Amsterdam, and we don't have anything like them in Holland."

We began to talk, first about Switzerland, then about

America and my work, and finally about her. I asked what kind of work she did.

"I'm a missionary mother," she said with a note of irony in her voice, as though she expected me to question her. And I almost did, because she didn't look like any missionary I had ever known. She was dressed in faded jeans and she looked like a tomboy.

After sizing me up for a few seconds, she began to laugh. "Oh, I'm not one of those *religious* missionaries," she said. "I'm a social worker. I work with disturbed children in Amsterdam. And my husband is a teacher in a school for troubled boys.

"Last week," she continued, "my husband and I were on an airplane, and a missionary sat down beside us. We talked as you and I are doing now and when we finished, she said that in a way we were like missionaries. I liked that idea. So I've begun to call myself a missionary mother."

Marijke went on talking about her life, her husband and their work. From nine to five, they worked at their professions. And when their offices closed in the evenings, they were substitute parents.

"For some kids," Marijke explained, "nine to five is not enough. Some children come from very bad homes where the parents do not treat them well. We take one or two of them at a time into our home for a month or two. We give them love, attention and discipline, try to let them see how a family can be when people care about each other and learn to share. It's helped the kids, and it's helped my husband and me. In some ways, we've grown as much as the kids."

I was impressed with her sincerity and enthusiasm, but I was puzzled by her apparent hostile attitude toward organized religion. Curious, I brought up the subject again. "Do you relate to a church in any way?"

"Not at all!" she said emphatically.

119

"You say that with such intense feeling," I ventured. "Any particular reason?"

She sighed with resignation, then spoke. "When my husband and I first married," she said, "we tried the church. But we discovered that most people were more interested in *talking* about helping people than in *doing* something about it. We have a desire to help make life better for others, so we left and haven't been back."

Her remark bothered me and set me to thinking. I couldn't deny that there was truth in what she had said. Church people often do a lot of talking about helping others. Perhaps one reason in that it's easier to talk about a problem than to do something about it, especially when doing means personal involvement and sacrifice. Yet Jesus instructed us to put His ideas and our God-given talents into action. When He said, "Follow me," he meant to get up and do what has to be done. If anyone is ever going to be an effective servant, a people builder, he must find ways to help others grow and live better.

There are as many effective ways to be people builders as there are people with needs. Angelo and Marijke and her husband are only a few examples but their lives illustrate a basic truth at the heart of the idea of people building. Every person, regardless of who he is, can help another person grow if he matches his skills and talents effectively to another person's needs. And in doing this, he also will grow!

CHAPTER 19

The Healing Power of Kindness

PAULA, A GOOD FRIEND OF MINE, recently told me of an experiment she and two friends tried when they were young and starting out together as secretaries in a New York engineering firm. They discovered that the touch of kindness can work miracles and transform relationships.

Paula is a quiet person who smiles frequently, a woman who possesses poise and self control. She never seems rushed. She always does her job promptly and efficiently.

When Paula and her two friends arrived at their new job they were assigned to desks in a large room with several other secretaries, most of whom had been with the firm for several years. Their reception was, as Paula described it, anything but warm. A few of the other secretaries looked up as the two young women entered and made their way to their desks. One of them said hello, but not one of them smiled.

Paula thought their behavior unusual, but brushed it aside and started to work. "Maybe it's a bad day, or maybe they're just busy," she rationalized. Still, their attitude disturbed her. She thought it unusual for anyone to simply ignore newcomers to an office staff.

Throughout the morning, Paula tried to keep her attention on her work but she couldn't help noticing how the secretaries reacted to one another. One of them asked another, who had apparently finished the work assigned to her, if she could type a letter which had to go out that day. The second girl snapped, "Look, I do my work and you do yours. I'm not paid to work for you."

At lunch the first day, Paula and her friends began to discuss their new job. "I do hope every day isn't like this one," one of them said. "I don't think I've ever seen a colder group of women in my life."

"I'll agree with that," the second said. "I overheard two of the secretaries complaining about another one and then about the engineers in the firm. What bothers me most is that I think they *wanted* me to hear what they said. There's a tremendous amount of hostility in this office."

The three continued to talk and generally agreed that since it was only the first day perhaps things would be better the next. However, things did not get better. Each day they became more aware of the underlying hostility which made everyone uncomfortable and hindered progress. The girls at last became discouraged.

"If we hadn't been in the office such a short time," one of Paula's friends said to her after about three weeks, "I'd quit."

"I feel that way, too," Paula said. "Let's have lunch and talk about it."

They went to lunch. And while they talked, they reached a decision which ultimately was to change the atmosphere of the entire office.

"I don't like to be a quitter and I know you don't

either," Paula said to her two friends. "I'm not much of a reformer either. But I don't enjoy misery, and that's exactly what everybody in the office has. They're all miserable because they're so unkind to each other. Then they're unkind because they are miserable. It's a vicious cycle. If only those women would start being kind to one another and learn to do their work without complaining, things would be different. They might even learn to like one another and to enjoy their work. Maybe if we try to be kind to them, even though they aren't kind to us, we might improve the place. And we might even help them."

The three girls agreed to try to be kind and helpful to the other secretaries. They would continue to work without complaining and when there was spare time they would offer to help the others.

At first, nothing happened, and the other secretaries continued to complain and gossip about each other. But Paula and her two friends did not give up.

One morning about a month after the three women began their experiment, one of the older secretaries came over to Paula's desk and said, "I heard Richard ask you to hurry and get that report out. My work is light this morning. Can I help?"

"Oh, would you?" Paula replied gratefully. "I would appreciate that so much." She handed the secretary a part of the report. She could hardly believe this was happening. The secretary took the report to her desk and began to type. Maybe the kindness experiment was beginning to pay off, Paula thought.

Similar incidents started to become more frequent and gradually the mood of the department began to change. By December, six months after Paula and her friends joined the firm, the atmosphere in the secretarial office was different. There were smiles and friendly chatter and a spirit of real cooperation.

At the staff Christmas party, the president of the firm

123

showed his appreciation of the change when he commented, "I don't know what's happened in this office, but everyone seems much happier lately. And what a difference it makes in our work!" Although he didn't know exactly what had happened, Paula and her two friends knew that it was the result of the transforming touch of kindness.

Johann Wolfgang von Goethe, the German poet and philosopher of the 18th century, wrote that kindness is the golden chain by which society is bound. Without sensitivity to other people's needs and the touch of kindness which endeavors to meet those needs, there can be no true society. There is only a group of individuals, each fending for himself without regard for the other. Without kindness there are no growing relationships in which people relate constructively to one another. Remarkably, it requires little effort to decide to behave kindly toward another person. It sometimes requires much more stamina to carry out that decision. Yet, when the relationship is important to us, kindness may be the very quality which can make the necessary difference. And a kind word or act will usually bring rewards far greater than the effort.

In a very different kind of situation I learned that kindness coupled with a measure of inner calm, can transform a drastic situation from a near crisis to one with a positive ending. This was a valuable lesson I learned from my secretary, Gerd Gunnulfsen.

One afternoon Muriel Boyle, the receptionist at the Marble Collegiate Church in New York City, called my office to say that a deeply troubled man had come into the church and was demanding to see a minister. The man was extremely agitated, she said, and she asked if someone could come down to the desk as soon as possible. All of the other ministers happened to be out of the building. In addition, I happened to be involved in something I considered no less urgent and could not leave just at that moment. Finally

Gerd decided she would go talk to the man herself.

An hour later she returned to tell me what had happened.

"Arthur," she told me, "that man was so nervous and angry when I walked into the room. He wanted to see a minister and he was not too happy to see me. I wasn't too happy to see him, either. He was pacing the floor, waving his arms and complaining loudly about everybody and everything. He was even complaining about himself. Right then, I think he hated the whole world and just needed to tell somebody how he felt."

"How did you handle him?" I asked her.

"I got quiet inside and talked to him in a very soft, gentle voice," she said. "I didn't oppose anything he said and I didn't agree with him, either. I just listened. After a few minutes, he began to calm down enough so that we could talk about what was really bothering him. By the time we finished he was no longer agitated. In fact, he thanked me for listening and then said he was going to walk home. He needed the exercise, he said."

Then Gerd looked me straight in the eye and said, "Maybe you preachers should slow down long enough to try the same technique sometime."

A few weeks later, I had the opportunity to try her suggestion. Dr. Norman Vincent Peale was conducting a memorial service in the Marble Collegiate Church for the late president of Taiwan, Chiang Kai Shek. The huge, imposing sanctuary was filled with people including dignitaries from several governments. When Dr. Peale began to speak, a woman sitting in the front row of a side balcony only a few feet above him began to clap her hands and to shout, "That's right, Norman! You say it!"

Within seconds, an usher started toward her. I was sure there would be a loud, disruptive scene. I stood nearby, so I motioned to the usher to wait. I walked to where the lady was and quietly sat down on the balcony step beside her. I made an effort to get quiet, as Gerd had done. Then I leaned over and whispered to her, "The next time you want to clap, do it this way." I moved my hands in a clapping motion without making a sound. She followed my example.

"And the next time you want to talk to Dr. Peale, do it like this." I moved my lips silently. To my surprise, she did exactly as I suggested.

When Dr. Peale concluded his remarks I whispered to her, "Why don't you come with me." Obedient, she got up and tiptoed behind me out of the sanctuary.

I would not have expected such an immediate and successful response to Gerd's suggestion, especially coming from a woman who, I later learned, had a long history of unstable and disruptive behavior. Although it may have had only a fleeting effect upon her, the quiet, gentle, kind approach had been exactly what the woman needed to calm her and to minimize a disruptive situation. Kindness, enforced by a spirit of inner calm, was like a healing balm for her. It was the transforming touch.

I was the person who benefited most from the incident, however. In those few minutes spent with this woman, I took another step in personal growth when I learned to use the resources within myself in a different way to establish a right relationship with another human being.

All of us need those moments of quiet, calm kindness. We need both to give them and to receive them. It is in such moments that souls and hearts touch and a bond of understanding is formed. Those are the moments when real growth begins and right relationships start to develop.

There are many ways to use kindness to help relationships. It is not necessary to wait until problems arise such as those I have described. An ordinary day can be transformed into a memorable one by a simple, loving gesture or a kind comment. One such incident happened just a few years ago.

On a very busy afternoon the telephone rang and my secretary, Gerd, said my wife was calling. Although I didn't really have time to talk, I thought it might be urgent, so I picked up the receiver.

"I called to say that thirteen years ago this minute we met for the first time," Gloria said. "And I'm so glad!"

When I hung up the telephone, I felt absolutely tremendous. Even today when I think about the call, I have the same warm, happy feeling. A few loving words made a big impression on me for a long time.

The quiet, gentle, kind touch can transform even the most angry and despondent person. It can calm a troubled soul and boost a sagging spirit. And it can do even more than that. Kindness, more than any other human quality, will help us to grow both individually and in our relationship with others. There is power in kindness—healing power.

CHAPTER 20

Let Us Give Thanks

WE CAN DO NO GREATER KINDNESS to ourselves and to others than to learn to be truly thankful. In the midst of all circumstances, both good and bad, there is always something for which we can give thanks.

One night my good friend Warren Delventhal was driving home behind a truck traveling near the Delaware Water Gap in New Jersey. Suddenly, for no apparent reason, the truck veered to the left, grazed the center divider in the road, flipped over and landed upside down in the empty oncoming traffic lane.

Warren slammed on his brakes, stopped his car on the shoulder of the road, got out and dashed across the road. As he neared the massive overturned truck, he thought the driver must surely be dead. The cab was crushed, the windshield smashed, the door caved in. Debris and cargo were strewn everywhere.

Warren leaned over to look into the cab of the truck and as he did, the driver came crawling out. The man's jacket was torn and blood oozed from a cut on his cheek.

"Are you all right?" Warren blurted, stunned to see the man alive.

The driver stood up, stared at the wreck for a moment and said repeatedly, "Thank God. Thank God."

At first, Warren couldn't understand. The driver had lost his truck and the cargo and must have been in pain from his injuries. However, instead of commenting on the loss or the injuries, the driver released the first thought that came to him in that dreadful moment: "I'm alive. Thank God." The truck driver was obviously a man who could find good in any situation.

William Law, an 18th-century English clergyman, once wrote about how edifying a grateful response can be, especially in time of calamity. Law believed that one of the surest ways to happiness is to make it a rule to thank and praise God no matter what happens.

Whatever happens to us, it can be turned into a blessing if we thank and praise God for it. Although we may feel the loss, we cannot build on it. We need only a little on which to build much.

Concentrating on what we do not have releases a destructive attitude which erodes our ability to appreciate what we do have. That attitude can be devastating in close relationships with others. It can lead to estrangement, loss of love and painful separation.

A physician I once knew lamented to me the divorce of his only daughter. She was in her early thirties and the mother of two chidren. "When Betty and Hal married," the father said, "there was so much promise for their life together, but they allowed it to fall apart. My wife and I tried to help them but we actually knew it was hopeless. Not once during the last two years of their marriage did I ever hear one of them compliment the other. When I talked to one of them, I heard only of the other person's short-comings, but I couldn't get either of them to admit that the other had any good qualities. And that could have made a difference. If only they had just looked for something to appreciate in each other, they might still be married and happy together."

That was twenty years ago, but with each passing day, I see more of the truth in the doctor's statement. Showing appreciation to another person builds life and helps bridge the gulf created by dissention. Showing gratitude to another person can help keep a positive, loving force alive in the midst of what might otherwise be a destructive situation.

Some time ago I was faced with the necessity of applying this positive philosophy to my own life. And it wasn't easy. A certain man who had often been critical of me one day confronted me with one of my weaknesses, and his words wounded me deeply. My initial reaction, of course, was anger. I immediately thought of all *his* weaknesses and I had no difficulty concluding that he had more of them than I did.

Later some close friends with whom I discussed the incident tried to comfort and reassure me, but the pain persisted. Whenever I saw the man I felt again the sting of his critical judgment and I experienced anger all over again. Each time I felt it, it seemed worse. Then one day as I was telling a friend about it, he asked me pointedly, "Is there any truth in his criticism?"

I had to admit, reluctantly of course, that there was.

"In that case, facing the truth should be good for you, shouldn't it?" he asked. Again, reluctantly, I had to admit he was right.

"Why don't you just swallow your pride, then, and

thank him for his criticism?" my friend said. "Tell him you see the truth in what he says and that you will strive for growth in the area of your weaknesses."

I decided to follow my friend's advice. The criticism had hurt, and I was still angry. Yet, after praying for strength to show some honest appreciation, I went to the man and told him that he had helped me with his comments and that I was grateful for them.

The man was as surprised to hear my words as I was to feel the truth of them in my heart. From that time we began to work on our negative feelings about each other until today our relationship is at last open, solid and mutually trusting.

That man taught me a useful lesson: No matter how much animosity there may be between two people, if one focuses on the positive traits of the other person, though they may be few and far between, and has the courage to say *thank you* or I *appreciate that* he can successfully break down strife and in its place sow peace and trust.

St. Paul appreciated the benefits of experiencing and showing gratitude. He never once forgot how Jesus had changed his life. He faced numerous conflicts with people and many dangerous situations. In the eleventh chapter of Second Corinthians, beginning with verse twenty-three, Paul wrote of beatings, imprisonment, shipwreck and hunger, plus daily pressure and anxiety from the churches he was striving to build. Despite all those difficulties, he was able to say in his letter to the Philippians, "I have learned in whatever state I am to be content. I know how to be abased, and I know how to abound; in any and all circumstances I have learned the secret of facing plenty and hunger, abundance and want. I can do all things in Him who strengthens me." (Philippians 4:11-13)

If we can learn to begin and end each day with a prayer

of thanksgiving on our lips — if we can endeavor to find, in ever situation, something to be truly thankful for — if we will cultivate and nurture a spirit of thankfulness for the blessing of life itself, our joy will be multiplied and we'll quickly find that we daily have even more for which to thank God.

CHAPTER 21

. . . As We Forgive Others

THERE IS NO WAY in which a person can grow mentally, emotionally or spiritually without being a forgiving person. Growth and forgiveness are inseparable. Certainly no relationship can grow or even survive without a forgiving attitude. Nothing can bring two people closer together than to experience genuine forgiveness. Yet, how hard it is for some people to forgive!

The unhappiest person I know is a woman I've known for twenty years. Every day she seems to become more miserable. Whenever we meet, our conversation usually shifts to some story about how someone has hurt her. It may have been yesterday or even twenty years ago—time does not seem to make a difference because she remembers each injury vividly. Through the years her relationships have deteriorated until by now she is virtually alone. She complains that no one loves her and she cannot understand why.

133

The key to her problem, however, is expressed in her frequently-repeated statement, "I'll never forgive—" If she ever honestly asks herself why she is not growing and why she is friendless and unhappy, she may discover that her decision to carry resentments and not forgive is at the root of her problem.

No one lives in a vacuum. We are social creatures. Our success in living relates directly to our ability to get along with others. Because we are only human, things will sometimes happen which hurt us. Yet, we do not have to carry resentment.

Jesus spoke clearly and explicitly about forgiveness and there is no mistaking His meaning. *Forgive us our wrongs,* He said, *as we forgive those who have wronged us.* How much must we forgive? *Seventy times seven*—or as many times as is necessary. *Love your enemies,* He said. *Pray for those who despitefully use you.* And when He was faced with the supreme test of His own teaching, He asked forgiveness for those who crucified Him. Even as men drove the nails through His hands and His feet Jesus prayed, "Father, forgive them. They do not know what they are doing." (Luke 23:24)

Regardless of the number or the severity of the offenses, we must forgive. We must not rationalize and look for excuses to harbor resentment. Jesus did not allow room for resentment because He understood how dangerous it is. He knew the destructive power of an unforgiving heart. When we do not forgive someone, we bind ourselves to that person in a negative bond. The unforgiveness retards growth and we find ourselves stuck at the level of hardness and meanness.

But how does a person forgive? What is the process?

Through the years I have found that there are three steps to forgiveness which have proved successful for many people. When we do all three consistently and make no exceptions, we become healthier, happier, freer and more loving.

The first step is to affirm forgiveness—to determine that we can and will be forgiving. Unless we believe that we can do this, no amount of persuasion from anyone else will make us more forgiving. We must think forgiveness and affirm it until it becomes so much a part of us that all negative and hostile feelings become alien. When we affirm forgiveness, it is not long until we are able to respond automatically to a painful thought or memory with an attitude of forgiveness.

The second step in forgiveness is based upon a sound principle of healing which says that a wound must be cleaned thoroughly in order to heal properly. Working through anger and guilt feelings is something very much like cleaning a wound because it removes the debris of resentment so that forgiveness can then take root and flourish.

It is not sufficient to say that we will just forget it when someone hurts us deeply. Deep hurts cannot be resolved so easily. When suppressed, they come to the surface in various ways, creating problems in our relationships and even causing illness. Indeed, medical experts have been able to observe and to document a connection between anger and resentment and the degenerative diseases of the body that is more than coincidental. Trying to suppress a hurt does not accomplish anything. On the contrary, it is usually a dangerous thing to do. The best way to handle a hurt is to admit it, verbalize and identify it and choose to let it be healed.

In the third and final step to forgiveness we accept the fact that the past is past and that we are living in the present. We recognize that although the pain belongs to the past, we can and will receive healing now. We cannot change what has happened but we *can* change our attitude

135

toward it, choosing to view the troubling event as a growing experience and giving thanks for what we can learn from it.

The rest of a wonderful life is ahead. We can live it tied to resentments from the past and be defeated. Or, with God's help, we can gain the release we need to move beyond the past and to live victoriously in the present. It's up to us to make the decision to forgive—and to stick to it!

CHAPTER 22

Alone Is Not Lonely

LONELINESS IS ONE OF THE GREATEST PROBLEMS of the 20th century, although it is not unique to our age. Since the beginning of time man has known the emptiness, the deep discomfiture of being separated or alienated from others, sometimes even when in the midst of people who care for him. In his effort to relieve that feeling of aloneness, he has reached out to others, and up to his Creator, seeking contact with another.

Although man's reaching out may ease some of his distress, it will never solve his problem. The answer to loneliness does not lie outside oneself, but within—for loneliness is a prison which can be unlocked only from the inside. Only the lonely person himself can open his own prison door.

Each of us at some time is alone and lonely. The novelist Thomas Wolfe wrote, "Which of us is not forever a stranger and alone?"

137

Recently I was asked to lead a discussion on loneliness for a group of middle-aged, single people at the Marble Collegiate Church. When I arrived, I was surprised to see the hall filled with people who had come from all over the city—people in the prime of life, active in careers and in outside interests. A hundred years ago, I thought as I observed the crowd, there would not have been more than half this number. Furthermore, I doubted that the topic of loneliness would have been of much interest. We must be doing something today to foster loneliness, I reasoned.

And certainly we do a number of things that contribute to loneliness. Our cities are filled with high-rise apartments which, although convenient and economical, don't foster a community spirit. A woman who was moving after twenty years in the same apartment remarked, "I came to know three or four people in this old fortress in all those years." She was not a cold person, and the building certainly was not anything like a fortress. She was merely expressing the most common condition of apartment dwellers—that of separation.

Her statement contrasted sharply with what another woman from a small, southern town told me not long ago. "Nearly everyone back home had a big front porch with a swing," she said. "In the evening when the sun set and the cool night breezes began to blow, we would sit on the porch and swing. There were my grandmother, my parents, my sister and sometimes an aunt or uncle. All the neighbors were in their swings, too, and we would talk across the porches. You couldn't see anyone, just some shadows moving back and forth in rhythm with the squeaking swings, but everyone was known by his voice."

Into our high-rise apartments we bring television sets which encourage individual viewing rather than communication. We have automatic dishwashers. There was a time when members of a family shared their secrets and their hopes as well as their problems while one washed and the other dried; now they just take turns loading the dishwasher. We've freed ourselves from labor, but also from built-in opportunities for sharing.

Furthermore, we are a mobile society. Approximately one in five American families moves every year. Moving provides excitement in new opportunities and expanded horizons but it creates another problem. Without roots, there is no feeling of belonging. We become like gypsies without the caravan. We move, but we leave the community behind.

An important part of the community is the older generation. A Jewish friend of mine, a New Yorker, lamenting the fact that both of his chldren had moved to California after marriage said, "Grandparents need the grandchildren, and the grandchildren need the grandparents. Unfortunately both have a common enemy—the parents." That man did not refer to family friction. He spoke of the modern tendency of everyone to do his own thing—live where he wants and do what he feels right for him. There is merit in that philosophy, but there is also a price. In this instance, it meant leaving the grandparents and a part of the family's heritage behind, creating loss and loneliness for all.

The mobility of people today also creates a destructive attitude in our relationships. Today's generations are part of a transient, disposable society. Much of the world is viewed in terms of *here today, gone tomorrow* and this attitude carries over into relationships.

One couple, representative of many I have known, came to me for counseling. They were unhappy and lonely because they had not found the closeness they had expected in marriage. They felt isolated from each other. As we explored their lives, we began to gain insights into their relationship. Each person came into the relationship fully expecting to lead his own life and to do his own thing while expecting the other to fill his need for physical and emotional intimacy. Each planned to get as much as possible from the relationship with minimal investment of self. Both had decided before marriage that if it did not work out as they hoped, they could easily get out of it.

Never had ever thought seriously about what is involved in building an intimate, happy relationship with another person. They didn't appreciate the fact that such a relationship begins with commitment of one's self to another and that without commitment there can be no honest giving and, consequently, no receiving. They didn't seem to understand that solid relationships require hard work. Building a life with another is never easy. And they didn't realize that a thing of value rarely if ever is attained without some suffering. That couple was prepared to enjoy the pleasures of a relationship, but they were reluctant to make themselves vulnerable to each other due to fear of being hurt.

Fortunately for this pair, they discovered that commitment also means working through problems so that both partners grow together. They found the way to fill the void in each other's lives when they learned that in any relationship, a person must get outside of himself and give in order to receive.

There is an old and fundamental spiritual law which says that the more you give, the more you will receive, and the more you will have to give again. This law still applies to all human endeavors, including the building of relationships. Loneliness is a state that can last as long as we make it last, and we must take the first step to conquer it by committing ourselves to someone or something which is beyond oneself. In so doing, we open the door to growth.

Seneca, a first-century Roman philosopher, wrote that we are born to live together. Society, he said, is an arch of stones, joined together, which would break down if each did not support the other. He had a point. Though every person needs some time alone, man is nevertheless a social animal. He hungers for meaningful, purposeful involvement with others and seeks to find it in an escape from loneliness.

Marjorie, the mother of a good friend of mine, was in her late sixties when she discovered how to deal with loneliness. When her children left home she soon realized she had more time to fill. Still, she wasn't lonely. There was work to be done, meals to prepare for her husband, Carl. She and Carl were devoted to each other and enjoyed spending their vacations and holidays visiting their children and grandchildren. Life continued much as it had since their marriage, but at a slower pace.

Then, shortly before their forty-second wedding anniversary, Carl suddenly died. His death was a tremendous blow to Marjorie. Everything which gave her security was suddenly gone. She and Carl had been close, and she had depended upon him for so much. He had always taken care of the finances and all of the other family business. She didn't even know how to write a check. Carl had always given her whatever she needed.

For weeks Marjorie didn't know what to do. She cried until she couldn't cry anymore. When her grief was nearly spent, she came face to face with the problem of going on alone, asked herself how to begin a new life. Her widowed sister encouraged her, but Marjorie knew that no one could give her the complete answer to her question. She would have to find it for herself.

Marjorie decided she would sell her house and take turns living with her son and daughter and their families. Both her children were concerned about their mother and were eager to do anything to see her happy again. Besides, having her around certainly helped with their babysitting needs.

That arrangement worked for a while, but the difference in the lifestyles of the two generations became a problem for all concerned. Arguments over how to rear the children, to manage the house, to run the kitchen caused tension and hard feelings. Marjorie knew her children loved her, but her living arrangment with them just wasn't working. She felt lonelier than ever.

At last she decided to rent a small apartment in a large complex where there were many young families. She would make new friends.She also enrolled in a driver's education course so that she could be more independent. Maybe a new setting without ties to the past was the answer to how to make a new start in life, she thought.

With so many young mothers and small children around her, Marjorie soon found herself babysitting, teaching mothers to sew and sharing ideas on cooking. Those were skills she had perfected during her forty-two years of marriage. Her neighbors came to love her, and before long there didn't seem to be enough hours in her day to do all that she needed and wanted to do.

Marjorie also joined a church in her new community. She and Carl had been active in their church before he died. Once again she began doing those things she knew and loved. She supervised church suppers, worked on committees and tended the nursery. Soon she was as indispensable there as she was in her apartment house.

One day as she sat reflecting about the changes in her life she wrote to her son, "I have learned that loneliness is something which can be solved only from the inside. When your dad died I wanted you and your sister to fill my life, but that was wrong. You have your families and your own lives. My loneliness was *my* problem, and I had to solve it myself. I had to decide what would make me happy and then do something about it. That was hard, as you know so well, but it was necessary. I could have been lonely the rest of my life if I hadn't made that decision."

Building a new life wasn't easy for Marjorie—nor is it easy for anyone else. On many occasions she shed tears of doubt and frustration and felt the temptation to return to her lonely shell. But when she decided that she did not want to be lonely all her life, she committed herself to reaching out to others. She cared for and supported those around her, and they reciprocated. The result was a life so filled with meaning and purpose that there was no longer any room for loneliness.

We, too, can escape the prison of loneliness, just as Marjorie did, by reaching out to others and finding new purpose and direction for our lives.

PART 5

How to Stretch Your Mind

But the wisdom that is from above is first pure, then peaceable, gentle, and easy to be entreated, full of mercy and good fruits, without partiality and without hypocrisy.

James 3:17

INTRODUCTION

We were swimming in the turquoise travertine pools at the foot of the Havusu Falls deep in Grand Canyon. Near the largest pool beneath the falls, some daredevil boys were swinging out of an enormous cottonwood tree and dropping into the water.

"That looks like a lot of fun," Gloria said. "Let's try it."

"Don't be silly," I said. "It's dangerous and if someone gets hurt we'll have a hard time getting help."

"Oh, I don't think we'll get hurt," she said. "The rope looks strong and the water is deep enough. Come on! Where's your sense of adventure?"

A few minutes later, whether I liked it or not, we were standing beside the cottonwood tree. Our youngest son, Chuck, was the first to go. He climbed out on a large limb, poised himself and then flew through the air, landing in the water with a splash. Our other son, Paul, followed. Then my wife grabbed the rope as the boys yelled, "Come on, Mom."

"Do you think you really ought to do that?" I asked. Gloria grinned and went flying through the air with amazing finesse and dropped into the water.

"Dad, it's your turn," Paul and Chuck yelled.

"No, I'd better not," I called back to them.

"Oh, come on, Art," my wife yelled. "There's nothing to it."

But I couldn't do it. I couldn't bring myself to jump out of that tree. For now I would be content to be accused of not having a sense of adventure.

While we were in the tree, someone we'd met was photographing the scene. When the film was developed we had three pictures of my wife and our two sons flying toward the blue waters of the pool on a rope and me clinging to the rough bark of the cottonwood tree, the rope clenched tightly in my hands.

Why did I refuse to swing out of the tree that day? I'd always had a sense of adventure. Why this sudden halt in the stretching process which adventure brings? I was afraid it might be an early sign of the winding down of living, pulling down the blinds and retreating from challenge. Disturbed by my attitude, I vowed to make an effort to reverse the process. I wasn't convinced that I should swing out on the next rope I saw hanging over a pond, but I believed I had to keep my mind open and get interested in the challenges I would be facing in the future. I told myself again that the purpose of life is to grow and to keep growing.

This disease, retreat from challenge, sneaks up on us. Sometimes it comes at an early age, often even before twenty. We want to order our lives, spiritually and mentally, and find neat answers to our problems. We want to keep the stresses and strains of living at a distance so that we can be comfortable. But that's one of the worse things a person can do. It's like closing down your mind, an action which can lead to stagnation. Truly, one of the great challenges of life is to keep growing.

Recently I was having dinner in a small restaurant in New Market, Virginia, a quiet town nestled in the beautiful Shenandoah Valley. While sitting alone and waiting for my dinner to arrive, I overheard this conversation between my waitress and a woman at the next table.

"I understand you will be graduating from high school this year," the woman said to the waitress. "What are you going to do after graduation?"

"I guess I'll go to college," replied the waitress.

"Are you looking forward to it?"

"Sometimes I do and sometimes I'm afraid of it," the waitress confessed. "College is supposed to be a lot of work, but I guess I want to get through it and get through my twenties. By then I should be on top of everything."

The woman smiled, wiped the catsup-smeared mouth of her little boy and then said, "Thirty isn't the age when you get settled. It's the time when you begin to figure what it's all about."

I, too, smiled. I'd wanted to say something to the waitress, but I didn't. It had all been said.

Yet, I could identify with the young waitress. For many years I had looked forward to the day when I would be on top of my situation — established professionally, secure in relationships and with enough money to do the things I wanted to do. I'd wondered why this wasn't happening as quickly as I thought it should. Then one day while listening to Dr. Peale discuss a problem he was facing I thought, "This is a huge problem. I can't imagine him ever facing a more difficult one." It had been a series of problems, one after another! "Why," I wondered, "does a man who has achieved so much and has so much ability have such problems?"

The answer emerged like the sun through the clouds.

Problems are a part of life. They're not signs of weakness nor are they necessarily bad. They are challenges, absolutely necessary if a person is to continue growing. They are people stretchers.

Several months ago at a dinner in the New York Hilton Hotel I sat next to the Chairman of the Board of one of America's largest banks. Somehow our conversation turned to people and to the way in which they view their personal problems.

"For a long time," the banker said, smiling, "I thought I would eventually get to the point in life where I would be on top of my problems. What a day it was when I realized that the greater my responsibilities, the bigger my problems —and that I would *never* get away from them, ever!"

My banker friend may never know how comforting I found his words to be. I have discovered that most people, at one point in their personal growth, have felt the same way he and I both did about problems. And that is most likely the reason why so many of us can remember the point in life at which our real growth began.

CHAPTER 23

Growing Never Stops!

FROM THE MOMENT WE FIRST SEE the light of day until we breathe our last breath and close our eyes to the world, our challenge and purpose in life is to keep on growing.

One of the advantages of being a minister at the Marble Collegiate Church in the middle of New York City is meeting and befriending many interesting and unusual people. Three of the most fascinating, most exciting men I know — Norman Vincent Peale, Amos Parrish and Homer Surbeck — are in their seventies and eighties. Every one of these men is in the age group that might be labeled *senior citizen*, yet people never think of them as such. They seem eternally young. Each of them is open to new and different ideas and each keeps on learning. Each looks ahead and plans for the future and also tries to make today count. Each maintains friendships with people he has known for years, yet each still makes new friends from among the younger generation.

Each of these men reads and travels and tries to understand the changing world even though he may disagree with some of the changes. Beyond those characteristics, which alone would make anyone interesting, these men are committed to someone greater than himself. Each puts his faith in God to work each day.

Not long ago I performed the wedding ceremony for one of these men, Amos Parrish. At the age of eighty, he married his seventy-eight-year old college sweetheart when, in the course of life's changes, each was single again. Shortly after the wedding, Amos was asked by a New York Times reporter for an interview for a series of articles on the decline that comes with aging. The eighty-year-old groom replied: "The answer is no! We are not on any decline. We're on an incline!"

Another man, typical of the three, was asked by a publisher to write a book on how to grow old gracefully. "What are you talking about?" he said to the publisher. "I'm not growing old. I'm still growing up!"

The lives of those dynamic men are in sharp contrast with the life of another man, the father of a close friend of mine. Frank, my friend, told me one day that his father had died. When I expressed my condolences, he replied that he did not feel the kind of sadness one would normally expect to feel at such a time. "My father is gone," he told me, "and I grieve for that. But I really mourned his death ten years ago."

I aked him what he meant.

"My father actually died ten years ago, when he stopped growing. His physical death now is only the formal ending."

That sad conversation was more than the mere sharing of grief because a man had died. It was the recognition of the disappointment which comes when a life is unfulfilled. At the time, Frank and I were students with everything in life seemingly ahead of us. Our heads were filled with ambitions and dreams. Yet, the words *he died ten years ago* had an impact. It was implicit in the long, heavy silence which followed that neither of us wanted our lives to end that way. And life doesn't have to end that way. Life can be rich and full to the last day.

Someone recently asked one of my octogenarian friends what he would like to have inscribed on his tombstone. After a moment of thoughtful silence he spoke. "Mind stretcher," he said. For all of his many years this man has tried to keep stretching his mind, knowing that it is one sure way to stay young and to keep growing. He is forever looking for new ideas and new people, new experiences and new understanding. Mind stretching is an activity which we can all practice, especially when we learn how important it is to our growth and learn to do it well.

Cardinal John Henry Newman, 19th Century English theologian and author, wrote: "Growing is the only evidence we have of life." There is no such thing as standing still. We either stretch and grow or we decline and decay. The dividends of growth are far greater than most of us can possibly imagine. Continued growth is not only essential to life but it pays off in many rich and rewarding ways!

CHAPTER 24

To Learn Is to Live

I AM SADDENED whenever I hear someone display little interest in learning more about life and about himself. To attempt the difficult and sometimes painful task of answering life's tough questions is a burden which some people would rather avoid. However, the person who shuns that task is usually a problem to himself as well as to others. He is turned inward instead of outward to life. An ancient philosopher once wrote, "This man of little learning grows old like an ox; his flesh increases, but not his wisdom."

On the other hand, I am always elated by the person whose eyes are open and whose mind is alert to opportunities for learning. He or she revels in the pleasures of learning, yet each learning experience seems to increase that person's humility. Sir Isaac Newton, the 17th century English philosopher and mathematician, was one of the most learned men of his day. Yet, late in life, he said, "I do not know what I may appear to the world; but to myself I seem to have been only like a boy playing on the seashore and diverting myself in now and then finding a smoother pebble or a prettier shell than ordinary, whilst the great ocean lay all undiscovered before me." Despite his expanding knowledge, Newton was humbled by the vastness of what he yet had to learn.

We must never stop learning. We can't afford to, for learning is the master key to growth. We must not be like the student who stops learning as soon as the degree is granted or when the last bell of the school year rings. Learning is a non-stop process which occurs within. And although it is facilitated by formal education, it is not dependent upon it. Learning is a personal, lifelong endeavor.

Before a recent presidential election, several historians were asked to identify America's greatest president. Abraham Lincoln was rated first, which is understandable because of his accomplishments, but remarkable because of his humble beginnings. Born in a log cabin in the backwoods, he received little schooling, the aggregate totaling only one year.

His education, however, was continuous as he mastered the limited resources available to him. He knew intimately only a few books—the Bible, Daniel Defoe's *Robinson Crusoe*, William Shakespeare's plays, John Bunyan's *Pilgrim's Progress*, Aesop's *Fables*, Weems's *Life of Washington*, and the *Autobiography of Benjamin Franklin*. Much of Lincoln's ability to express his ideas clearly and eloquently and his ability to comprehend the meaning of greatness can be traced to those books. In spite of the paucity of his formal education, Lincoln became a thinking giant. He took full advantage of his opportunities and made learning a life-long endeavor—an example of the way life should be lived.

One of my favorite examples of how we can learn from

the world around us comes from George Washington Carver, the brilliant Negro botanist who is best remembered for discovering so many ways to use the peanut. Early in the 20th century when the boll weevil threatened to ruin the cotton industry and with it the economy of the South, Carver advised planters to plant crops which would provide income without sustaining the boll weevil population. He told them to alternate their annual crop of cotton with a crop of peanuts and sweet potatoes. The planters did as he recommended only to find that they had peanuts when there was no market for them. One planter approached Carver and asked what to do. Carver didn't have an immediate answer, but he was determined to find one.

He went to his laboratory, which he called "God's Little Workshop," and asked the Heavenly Father to help him solve the problem of the people, whom he had advised to plant peanuts. Then he began to analyze the peanut. He took it apart, heated, pressurized it, and mixed it with other substances. Day after day and week after week he worked in his laboratory—and eventually he came up with hundreds of different products. The little old peanut gave people a better diet and a new industry, and helped revolutionize the economy of the South.

Somebody once asked Carver how he had managed to discover so much. "I really discover nothing," he replied. "I come into my lab and I'm lost." "But," he said, "I can do all things through Christ. I am His agent. With my prayers I mix my labors, and sometimes God is pleased to bless the results."

George Washington Carver was not too different from other people in many respects. Although he possessed great native intelligence and was persistent with his work, the system he used to solve his problems is one that we all can use. He would not limit God. Instead, through Christ, he received God's infinite wisdom in order to solve his own problems. There is much to be learned even from the smallest of things—including peanuts—but we have to want to learn and then be ready to take advantage of our opportunities.

One of the most remarkable women I know when in her fifties left a successful teaching career and returned to school to complete her doctorate. When she finished, a prestigious eastern university asked her to be the chairman of one of its departments. She had never done that kind of work before and at first she questioned her ability. Still, she was excited by the challenge and finally accepted.

Shortly after assuming her new post, she was diagnosed as having cancer and underwent immediate surgery. The experience was devastating. It seemed then that everything she had worked so hard to accomplish would never be realized. Yet she returned to work. Then the second blow came another severe illness, and recovery did not occur this time for several months. She returned to the hospital, then went home until she could get back her strength.

When it seemed she was regaining her health, she received a third blow—a second operation was needed. She was extremely discouraged, but still was not ready to give up. "I haven't worked hard all these years preparing myself for my job only to give up now. I can't and I won't." Again she returned to her job, and fortunately has had no further illnesses.

Later, at sixty-three, this woman faced mandatory retirement in two years. Knowing herself, she did not imagine it would be easy for her. Yet, the experiences of the past few years had helped her to grow more than ever before. She had worked hard to become a success in her career. And now she was going to work to be a success in retirement. "I'm going to plan it and really do something with it," she announced.

During vacations and holidays, she began to look

around the country for just the right place to retire. She wanted a town with a stimulating environment, a good library and a vital, active church. She eventually found such a place, but the town posed an unexpected problem for her. She couldn't drive, and there was no way that she could live comfortably there without a car. Returning home, she immediately enrolled in driving and automobile maintenance classes.

For the first few months after this lady retired she sent her friends cheerful letters describing her various experiences. Then, after a while no one heard much from her. When at last they inquired about her, they learned what had happened.

During the first year in her new home, despite the fact that the people in the community had welcomed her, she'd run into some distressing realities in her new way of life. Without a job to go to each day and colleagues to associate with, she suddenly became aware that she would have to learn to relate to people in a different way. These people were not colleagues, but friends—and they had children. She had never been around children much, but she found a cooky jar helped. There were other things to learn— gardening, maintaining a house, a whole new life style. Her friends found that in all her new learning experiences she had merely fallen behind in her letter writing.

I saw this lady again recently. As I had anticipated, she is lively, enthusiastic and extremely happy, advanced in years but still young in heart. She realizes that the purpose of all of life is to continue to grow each day. She knows, too, that without learning, growth is impossible.

CHAPTER 25

What Do You Think?

OF ALL ENDEAVORS essential to growth, none is more important than that of thinking. Yet, thinking has a rather poor reputation. "Five percent of the people think," someone once said. "Ten percent *think* they think; and the rest would rather *die* than think." Henry David Thoreau wrote, "The millions are awake enough for physical labor, but only one in a million is awake enough for effective intellectual exertion; only one in a hundred million to a poetic or divine life. To be awake is to be alive."

Long before Thoreau, an unnamed ancient writer expressed similar sentiments when he said sardonically, "Learn to think. It will profit you well, for there is so little competition."

These may be exaggerations, but they point up an important lack among us. They all indicate that most people do not use and develop one of their most important

159

resources—the ability to think. And they offer encouragement for those who are willing to put forth the extra effort to improve themselves. Several years ago, when we were traveling in South America, Gloria and I discovered a mixup in our departure tickets for the balance of our trip. We had accidentally been scheduled to leave on different days, the boys and I first, then Gloria. Of course we had intended to leave together so I called the travel agent at once and told him the problem.

He wasn't much help. "There are few flights in and out of this country and all of the reservations are filled," he said. "You cannot leave on the same plane."

We had planned too long for this trip to give up on the first try. Gloria and I and our two sons hurried over to the travel bureau, which was exactly what I pictured such a place to look like. It was located in a wooden building with a tin roof and peeling paint. The inside would have been unbearably hot in the tropical heat had it not been for an immense shade tree which rose straight up from hard-packed dirt. We pushed our way through the door and entered a room filled with people — women in loose-fitting cotton print dresses, little children holding fast to their mothers' skirts.

And there, behind a counter, was the travel agent. His face matched the languor which everyone felt. With movements synchronized to the slow rotation of the fan which hung from the high ceiling, he shook his head back and forth in an answer to all inquiries and repeated, "No, it is impossible." Every answer was no. There were no flights available. At last we made our way to the counter, and the travel agent wiped his brow and said, "No it's not possible for you, either."

Since there didn't seem to be much hope in that place, we left and went directly from the travel agent to the KLM Airline Office, where we thought there might be a little more effort to solve our problem. Inside the office, we found a similar scene — long lines of people, and ticket agents who moved their heads in the same methodical manner as the travel agent.

I looked behind the counter and found a petite young woman who, unaffected by the outside heat in this air-conditioned office, seemed alert and full of life. I caught the eye of this vivacious brunette and asked if I might speak to her. She nodded. "Would you kindly help me think through a problem?" I asked persuasively.

She smiled, perhaps because she did not get many requests to think through problems, and said she would help. She listened with alert interest as I spelled out the details of our awkward situation, her eyes never leaving mine.

"As it stands now," she said at last, "there is no way all of you can be on that plane in two days. But if you'll come back in the morning about ten o'clock, I'll see if there are any changes."

At ten o'clock the next morning, we were standing at the ticket counter only to find there were no changes. "Don't give up," she said. "Come back at four this afternoon."

Back at four, and *still* there were no changes. But I could tell from her expression that she had an idea. And it might pay off. "Get to the airport early tomorrow morning," she said. "Be the first there and make yourselves obvious to the officials. Stay together as a family. I'm sure they won't separate a family, especially if it means leaving the mother behind."

We prepared to do as she suggested. Then late that night the phone rang and when I answered I recognized the young lady's voice. "Your wife has a reservation on the flight with you and your boys," she said. The problem was solved. She had been only one person in the crowd, yet she was outstanding because she had dared to think and then to act.

Jesus was a thinker. He was in a community where people held to age-old traditions, allowed themselves to be suppressed by the legalisms of their past. Creative thinking had little acceptance. But He encouraged and challenged people to use their minds, to really think about some of the traditions which stifled them. One such tradition was the observance of the Sabbath. The law said that no one should be healed on the Sabbath. Such a law was contrary to common sense for it conflicted with God's loving concern for people. Why *not* heal on the Sabbath? So Jesus raised the question, "Was the Sabbath made for people or were people made for the Sabbath?"

Jesus was thinking. *It doesn't make sense,* He reasoned, *for a tradition to take precedence over the health of a sick person. Let's get things in perspective. The Sabbath was made for people! Human beings are God's most valued creation. Why allow a man's well-being to be overruled by a thoughtless tradition?* Then Jesus took courage with His thinking, healed the sick man and made a creative change as He challenged stifling traditions.

There are a multitude of problems and many doors of challenge and enlightenment that await the thinker. The purpose of life is growth, and we grow only when we learn to think intelligently and imaginatively. The rewards are tremendous!

CHAPTER 26

Can You Imagine!

CREATIVE THINKING CAN ADD DEPTH and meaning to your life. But if you want to add some excitement to your personal growth, learn to use your imagination. Keep it stirred up. Let there be no limits to healthy thinking and imagining.

One July day we were driving through Kansas where the sky and the land seem to extend forever and my wife said, "Look at that horizon. I wonder how far we can see."

That was an intriguing question, so I picked a spot as far away as we could see and then measured the distance to it with our odometer. It was thirteen miles in one direction. Next we wondered how vast an area we could survey. With the help of my son Paul who had just finished his first year of geometry, we figured we were surveying a circle 81.6 miles in circumference. Now, that seemed like a lot of territory, but our next figure was even more staggering. We were looking out across 520.6 square miles of rich, golden wheat, bending ever so gently in the warm breeze. The vastness made an impression on each of us.

"When you can see for miles as we are doing right now," Gloria said, "it makes you wonder how people can be so provincial in their thinking. This horizon is limited, but the mind's horizon is infinite."

Rachel Carson, the biologist who wrote *Silent Spring* and helped stir the nation's conscience about ecology, put imagination in the same category as wonder. She said that if it were possible she would give all children a sense of wonder so indestructible that it would last throughout their lives. That sense of wonder, she said, would be an unfailing antidote to boredom and disenchantment when in later years those grown-up children become preoccupied with things material and artificial, and alienated from the basic essence of life.

Once on a school holiday I took my sons Paul and Chuck and our neighbors, Scott and Stephen MacGuffie on a ride through the Connecticut countryside, traveling up the Merrit Parkway. Narrower than most modern superhighways the parkway is lined on each side by carefully-manicured grass and lovely trees of every kind for the most of its thirty-seven miles. Noticing the trees down the median, one of the boys remarked, "Wouldn't it be great if all highways had trees in the center so that at night you wouldn't be blinded by the headlights of other cars?"

Everyone agreed that it would. Then I asked them all a question. "Other than with trees, how do you think the problem of bright headlights might be solved?"

Four young minds went to work. I could almost hear them go into gear, preparing to turn out a stream of ideas. Within minutes, there were a dozen suggestions for solving the problem. They suggested diffused lighting, tinted glass, better mechanical dimming devices and many other ideas. Finally four-year-old Stephen asked, "Why do they make lights so bright in the first place?" He'd gone right to the heart of the problem, hitting the bull's eye.

Why try to solve the problem by treating the effects when you can go right to the cause?

I don't know if anything those boys suggested is even close to the eventual solution, but that is not important. The thing that impressed me most was their attitude. They never for one moment thought they might not be able to solve the problem! They didn't know the meaning of *impossible* and so they confidently dared to use their vivid and fertile imaginations!

Simple problems are frequently solved with a little imagination. And aren't most of our problems simple and even insignificant when we clear away the clutter which surrounds them? If imagination can work in small things, think what it can do when we are confronted with big problems. When we learn to think imaginatively, we can't help moving ahead, wherever we are. Instead of boxing ourselves in with stale ideas we need to let our imaginations soar and thereby add excitement to our thinking.

An executive of Macy's, the huge and famous New York department store, once told me how the store's president stretches people's minds and makes them think imaginatively. Once, during an executive meeting, the president told the group, "Let's suppose the world were about to be flooded. Every hill, mountain, continent, everything would be under water. What would you do?"

Three of the men began discussing the impending disaster. One said he'd be depressed and since there didn't seem to be much he could do, he would prepare to die. Another said he also would be worried and discouraged, but he would pray. The third said he'd be as concerned as the two others, but he was more imaginative. "I would figure out a way to live under water," he said.

Imaginative thinking makes great things happen. Didn't Jesus Himself challenge us to use our imaginations? Has anyone ever been more creative than He was in solving life's problems? Jesus questioned the way things were and challenged them—and we can, too!

CHAPTER 27

Thank God for Problems— Really!

ALTHOUGH WE THINK AND USE our imagination, many of us are nevertheless overwhelmed by problems. We tend to think of problems as burdens which weigh us down. We build and stack up our problems together in one big emotional hurdle, and we see no way of jumping over it.

Such thinking is self-defeating. A more constructive idea is to realize that the tougher the problem, the greater the opportunity for growth. The Apostle Paul promised us that God will not allow anything to come to us that we can't handle. Problems can be opportunities if they are seen as people stretchers and not as obstacles. Problems are given to us so that in solving them we can grow in strength and in maturity.

Some time ago I had an interesting conversation with a young man who was beginning to learn about the growth potential in his various problems. "Read this and tell me if I have a chance," said twenty-three-year-old George, a tall, dark-haired, athletically built young man.

"What is it?" I asked.

"It's a *Dear John* letter from my fiancée," he answered. "Just tell me I still have a chance."

I read the letter, and his fiancée seemed adamant. She'd had a change of heart. She saw no future in their relationship and said clearly and directly that it was over.

"How do *you* interpret it?" I asked.

"It's over, isn't it?" he said.

"It looks that way," I answered. "Has this ever happened to you before?"

"Never," he said. "I've been lucky. I have always been the one to end a romance. I was always in the driver's seat. It really hurts to be on the other end."

We talked for a while, during which time I shared my feelings of a similar experience in my own life. Then I asked, "Have you told your dad yet?"

"I just called him." George said forlornly.

"What did he say?"

"Dad sympathized with me and then said something which I know is true, but I sure didn't want to hear it."

"What is that?" I asked, curious.

" 'George,' he said, 'this experience could be the greatest opportunity yet to learn about yourself and to grow. We are tested by the dead-ends of life.' "

George experienced the frustration which each of us knows when we are confronted with seemingly insurmountable obstacles or when our goals are thwarted. Instead of giving us what we believe to be right for us, life sometimes says no.

Life is full of *no's*. They present themselves as a missed opportunity, a loss through death, a broken relationship, the loss of something valued or the failure to achieve a goal. And we grieve, because grief is a natural and healthy response to such disappointments.

Yet, think of what life would be like without problems. We might say it would be wonderful. But would it? A lawyer I knew once said he had envisioned all of his cases being closed. Everything was done: all letters answered, all calls placed, his office in perfect order. As he pictured himself in such a perfectly arranged environment, his whole idea of order and constancy suddenly changed. "That kind of situation would be paradise for a while," he admitted, "but then do you know what I think it would be? It would be just the way I've envisioned hell — a vacuum in which nothing ever happens." He shook his head and smiled. "I have to have some challenges to keep me going."

On a warm June afternoon a few days before school was to end for the year, my son Paul, then twelve, walked into my study. Paul was usually an energetic bundle of activity but on this day he was pensive and somber. His head was hanging and the usual sparkle in his eyes was gone.

"Hi, Dad," he said.

"Hi, Paul," I replied, and then waited for him to say what was on his mind. He was silent for a long time. Finally I asked, "Paul, what's bothering you? You look low. Is something wrong?"

He nodded. "I just came from school. We had the final assembly of the year. That's the one where the principal gives out the awards. I really wanted to win the science award," he confessed. "I worked hard all year. In fact, I got an A in science. I did extra projects and showed a lot of interest in the course. All year long I had pictured it in my mind. The principal would call my name and I would walk to the stage and get the prize in front of all my friends." He paused, then went on, "But I didn't get the award." He started to bite his lip, which had begun to quiver. He was fighting back the tears and I felt like crying myself when I saw his disappointment.

"Paul, who got the science award?" I asked.

169

He named the student and I waited for some remark about how unfair it seemed, but there was none. Paul was not going to put down anyone else in order to make himself feel better.

"Did he deserve to win?" I asked.

"I guess so, Dad," he said. "He made about the same grades as I did. I shook his hand and congratulated him. But it really hurt. I wanted to win that prize more than anything in the world." Then he suddenly brightened. "Do you think the people in the high school will let me sit in on a science class during the summer session? Maybe I can learn a lot and then I can win the award next year."

Problems have various effects upon people. Some people deteriorate or even dry up. Others grow, and some even become great. I like to think that Paul will grow in the years ahead from his disappointments. He knows who he is and what he has to offer, and when there is defeat, he is willing to try even harder. As long as he keeps seeing problems as people stretchers, he will grow right and strong.

Sidney, a dear friend of mine who has had a successful career with the same firm for thirty-five years, has spent the past five years locked in a relationship he has described as a thorn in his flesh. One of the great gifts Sidney possesses is his ability to relate well to other people. Because of that ability he was assigned to work with an executive of unusual business skill who nevertheless possesses a nasty, demanding, hateful dispostion which alienates him from others in the firm. One afternoon as Sidney and I discussed his job, I asked him how he could stay in such a bad situation. "Why don't you quit and find something else?" I suggested.

He couldn't quit, he said, and his reasons were understandable — his age, his pension and his personal investment in the firm.

"Why don't you ask for a transfer?" I asked. "You've been with the firm long enough to have your request honored."

"I've tried that route several times, Art," he explained, "but the senior officers claim I'm the only one who can work with this man and he is important to the company." Then Sidney shared some interesting discoveries he had made. "I've suffered through this problem," he said, "but I've gained something, too. If I didn't have the problem, I wouldn't have done half the praying I've learned to do. And it's made a big difference. I've had some interesting answers to my prayers, too. One of them is a better understanding of my boss. Oh, that doesn't mean I like the way he behaves any better, but I have begun to look beneath the surface at the real person. I learned that several years ago he had an operation which partially handicapped him and has helped to make him the way he is now.

"He, too, has a thorn in the flesh and his is even greater than mine. I leave mine at five o'clock each day but he takes his wherever he goes. Also, my increased prayer life has changed some other things — the way I view my family and myself, for example. One important thing I've learned from prayer is that there is grace enough to meet every need, and then some."

When we learn to see each new problem as a challenge rather than as an obstacle — when we learn the benefits of creative problem solving — we begin to realize that problems are usually only blessings in disguise and stimulants to growth. Indeed, there can be no progress without opposition. Without hurdles to scramble over, there are no victories. We need something to *overcome*, for it is in overcoming that we grow!

CHAPTER 28

Decide to Be Happy!

THE MOST SOUGHT-AFTER and elusive quality in life is un-doubtedly that of happiness. Everybody wants it and so few seem to find it. The search is often frustrating and disappointing. I wonder how many people know how rela-tively simple it is to get started on the road to happiness? It may be much easier than one might think.

Sue was a young woman who had a friend she ad-mired deeply. The friend, Alice, was a slightly-built, seventy-five-year-old woman who always seemed to be smiling and who could find something good and helpful in every situation.

"I don't know how she does it," Sue commented about Alice. "She has arthritis in her hands and they must hurt her most of the time. She'd still adjusting to being a widow. And I suspect she has financial problems. Yet she is so cheery. She hums and sings most of the time. She's so happy!"

Because she realized how the ups and downs in her own life seemed to dictate how she felt at different times, Sue finally asked Alice one day, "How can you always be so happy? I want to be happy, but it seems as if happiness is always beyond me."

Alice smiled and her bright, blue eyes seemed to look off into the distance for a moment. "I learned the secret from my father when I was a young girl," she said at last. "I was complaining one day about not being happy and he took my hand and pulled me over to him, his big arm around my waist. 'Alice,' he told me, 'you can't expect happiness to just happen. It doesn't work that way. You have to do something to make yourself happy. You're living each day as if happiness belongs to tomorrow. It doesn't. God wants you to be happy. If you're going to be happy you must decide to be happy right now. Don't put it off until tomorrow.'

"He got the message across to me, and since then I've tried to do what he said. My present happiness is the result. Long ago I decided that regardless of what happened I was going to be happy. I have been, and I still am."

Sue went away from that visit with a different outlook. She had learned a valuable secret and she resolved to apply it to her own life.

The secret of happiness which Alice shared had also been discovered by the Belgian theologian, priest and writer, Louis Evely. The reason so many people do not find happiness, Father Evely said, is that they do not know where to look for it. Too many people make the mistake of seeking one more material thing, one more pay raise, one more promotion, one more problem solved, one more handicap overcome. "If only I had that," they often say, "I would be happy."

For such people—and so many of us are guilty, too—happiness is always just out of reach. After one illness is gone there may be another. When one promotion is obtained there is another position which looks even more attractive. When we have more money, we spend more and find that there is still not enough.

Most of the problems which keep us from being happy can recur tomorrow. Still, happiness need not be always just around the corner. We can achieve it today—if we really want to. And if we are ever going to be happy, now is the time. We must decide to be happy right now. And we can be. Here's how.

Happiness is a state of mind which begins when we decide we want to be happy and are willing to learn how. We are not likely to be happy by accident for very long although we may experience some unexpected pleasures. We will be happy only when we understand that happiness is a matter of choice.

And so the first thing we do is decide to be happy now, just as Alice did. We don't wait for tomorrow. If we do, we'll discover that tomorrow has a way of never arriving. Once we've made that happy decision, we will begin to feel better, because we are taking charge of ourselves. Soon we will also have begun new growth as a vital and attractive person.

When we are happy, we grow because of our open-minded attitude. We look for the good in everything. We turn negatives into positives. We create a mental and emotional climate which fosters growth in mind and spirit. As happy, positive people, we will begin to affect others. And we'll find ourselves attracting experiences and people who stimulate additional growth, additional happiness.

Recently I met an airline stewardess who was radiantly alive, a pretty girl with a glowing vitality and lovely red hair which hung gently to her shoulders. She was so full of enthusiasm that after a while I stopped her as she came down the aisle and asked, "Are you always so happy?"

She gave me an enthusiastic smile. "Most of the time," she admitted frankly.

I found myself smiling back at her. "How do you do it," I asked, "with all the problems and all the problem people you have to deal with?"

She tossed back her long red hair. "Well, I've seen so many people hanging their heads and looking sad and glum. They would complain about how bad things were, what an awful day they were having, and I would find myself getting caught up in the same negative mood. It bothered me. So I asked myself if it were really necessary.

Right away I answered my own question. It wasn't necessary at all. I could and should be in control of my own moods. *I* could decide whether I would have a good day. From then on, I decided that every day would be a good day—and believe it or not, most of them are!" Then she added "I'm a Christian. It makes a big difference. God enables me to maintain a good attitude."

What she'd said made a lot of sense. No one ever *finds* a good day. We *make* a good day! God will help and inspire us to do it, but we must first be willing and determined!

We must also learn the art of being aware of every moment. In *Our Town*, Thornton Wilder's play about small-town life in New England at the turn of the century, Emily, a young mother who has died and is now observing life on earth, asks, "Do any human beings ever realize life while they live it—every, every minute?" Another character in the play replies, "No." He pauses, then adds, "The saints and the poets, they do some."

Why the saints and poets? What do they have or do that makes life's moments special? The ability to live every moment, rather than simply pass time is a rare human quality. Yet there are some ordinary people—not just saints and poets—who have that ability. I can think of several.

One of those people is the late Louis Kohler, a tall,

whitehaired Swiss gentleman with deep blue eyes and cheeks red from many years in the crisp mountain air of his native land. Louis, an artist, is the father-in-law of my younger brother, Ernest.

One evening shortly before he was to return to Swtizerland after spending a good part of the summer on the Maine island where we have a summer cottage, Louis came to our house for dinner. When we were seated at the table, Gloria placed a huge platter of steaming red lobsters in front of him. "Here's a special treat for a very special person," she said, smiling. "They were pulled from the water in that bay only twenty minutes ago." She pointed to the blue ocean which could be seen from our front door.

"Ah!" Louis exclaimed reaching for a lobster. He looked at it carefully, as though making a mental picture to recall at some future moment. At last he tucked his lobster bib under his chin and with a smile of great satisfaction, broke off a claw. He reached into the claw with a fork, extracted a tender morsel of pink meat, swirled it in melted butter, and then put the meat into his mouth and held it there, savoring every bit of the sweet taste. "Oh, this is good!" he said, at last sighing and leaning back in his chair. "Yes, this is very good!"

Slowly, Louis ate each bite as if it alone held something special which none other could provide. He did not simply eat his dinner, he *experienced* it.

After dinner, as we sat on the porch having our coffee and watching the sun set, we talked about Louis' many hikes around the island. "Do you remember those little blue flowers we saw in the field yesterday?" he asked Gloria.

"The wild chickory," she said. "Isn't it lovely?"

"When you see it again," he told her, "notice how pink the buds are before they open and how the stems are colored red." Louis had watched the plants grow and had, in his short stay, learned more about the island than most of the regular visitors know after coming there for years.

Louis made his discoveries by doing something which most of us are too hurried to do. He took the time to feel, smell, see and enjoy nature. He knew the wonderful characteristics of the various wildflowers, and how the North Atlantic's cold water looked when the waves broke upon the shore's gray, granite rocks in a fury of white spray. All of nature's treasures were his to enjoy, to remember.

"Louis," Gloria said, "I still get excited when I think about the blue herons we saw in the pond on the other side of the island."

Louis smiled. "Now, *I* have a surprise for *you*," he said to Gloria as he arose and walked into the living room, returning with a package. I could tell by Gloria's expression that she was hoping it would be one of Louis' beautiful watercolors.

Gloria eagerly opened the package and was pleased to discover a watercolor of a great blue heron standing in the pond. The subtle shading of the feathers said as clearly as any words that Louis had noticed every detail. Through his senses and his ability to capture the scene on canvas, he'd lived the moment to the fullest.

Today that painting hangs in our bedroom. It is the last thing I see before turning out the light and the first thing I see each morning. Every time I look at it, I think of Louis and I remember to try to live as he does—enjoying each moment as it comes.

This is possible when we relax and open our senses to the world around us, when we grow with the life we can see and hear and feel around us as we stop, observe and absorb. In pausing to drink in the color of the evening sky or the beauty of a friend's smile, the sound of children in the playground or the crunch of feet on crusted snow, to appreciate the gentle touch of a caring hand or to admire the sharp, angular lines of a skyscraper silhouetted against the sky at dusk, we live. In coming fully alive to the multitude of sights and sounds and feelings that God gives us to enhance our moments and our days, we begin to grow. And in growing, we learn to make our lives count!

A NOTE TO THE READER

These books were selected by the same editors who prepare *Guideposts*, a monthly magazine filled with true stories of people's adventures in faith.

If you have found inspiration in these books, we think you'll find monthly help and inspiration in the exciting stories that appear in our magazine.

Guideposts is not sold on the newsstand. It's available by subscription only. And subscribing is easy. All you have to do is write Guideposts Associates, Inc., Carmel, New York 10512. A year's subscription costs only $4.95 in the United States, $5.95 in Canada and overseas.

When you subscribe, each month you can count on receiving exciting new evidence of God's presence and His abiding love for His people.